Practical Guide
to
Curriculum and Instruction

PRACTICAL GUIDE

TO

CURRICULUM AND INSTRUCTION

by

Charles T. Christine

and

Dorothy W. Christine

PARKER PUBLISHING COMPANY, INC.

West Nyack, N.Y.

© 1971, *by*

PARKER PUBLISHING COMPANY, INC.

West Nyack, N. Y.

Library of Congress
Catalog Card Number: 70-161449

Printed in the United States of America
ISBN-0-13-690891-8
B & P

Dedicated to all men and women
who are proud to be called
teacher.

Why We Wrote This Book

This is a book about what to teach and how to teach it. It is intended for school administrators, teachers, curriculum supervisors, directors of instruction, and principals who are in need of a professional, straight-forward approach to building and maintaining a rational curriculum, and to improving instruction.

A plethora of books dealing with curriculum and instruction weighs on the bibliographies of education. One group of these is theoretically oriented toward scholars in the field, and while understandable to the practicing schoolman, offers little of practical value to immediate use. Another group of curriculum and instruction publications is intended to introduce undergraduate students to the literature of teaching. Such material is highly practical for introducing students and student teachers to the history and language of education, but this collection holds little that is new to the practicing educator.

This book, then, fills the void between the elementary and the highly theoretical works now in print. It is assumed that readers of this book both speak the language of the school house and are actively engaged in direct contact with pupils or teachers.

You will not find a theoretical approach to curriculum in this book. Chapter 2 deals with curriculum theory on a professional level, but the conclusion reached will surprise some professionals.

You will find a definition of *methods* in this book. Teachers of teachers have used the term *methods* for a long time, but few of them have communicated what they meant. This book takes inventory of the methods.

Practical approaches to school work have recently overconcentrated upon different ways to divide children and teachers. Team organizations, ungraded primaries, ungraded high schools, primary units, middle schools, modular scheduling plans, tracking schemes, and variations of the Joplin Plan jam our literature. This book deals with the problem of what to do with the learners after they have been grouped, graded, massed, or atomized.

You have read of simulation, programmed instruction, inter-action analysis, and possibly of systems approaches to curriculum and instruction. This book will help you decide whether or not any, or all, of these are for your class or school.

The real business of school people is deciding what to teach and how to teach it. It is too often true in the school house that the curriculum and instruction, concerns are buried beneath discussions of how to divide the students, how to deal with the school board, how to raise taxes, or (heaven help us) how to clean the floors. This book treats the central school issue—what to teach and how to teach it.

Charles and Dorothy Christine

Acknowledgements

We express our appreciation to the authors and publishers who kindly consented to allow us to reproduce copyrighted materials. These include Dr. G. A. Beauchamp, Dr. N. A. Flanders, Dr. J. I. Goodlad, Dr. Fred Kerlinger, Holt, Rinehart and Winston, The Kagg Press, and W. C. Brown Company.

We thank Mr. Bob Crilly of Newark Ohio, for his work in conceiving and drawing Figure 7-2.

Most authors express appreciation to a large number of former teachers and associates for ideas and idea stimulation. We too acknowledge that the writing of this book was so inspired and guided. However, we must acknowledge specific and direct aid and stimulation from Dr. J. K. Duncan and Dr. P. Klohr of Ohio State University, and from the fine teachers of Abington, Pennsylvania; Ardsley, New York; Edgemont, New York; Newark, Ohio; and the Westchester (New York) Cooperative Curriculum Council.

For technical help in writing the ADP section of Chapter 7 we thank Mr. Dick Gale of IBM, Columbus, and Mr. Len Boreski of IBM, New York.

For technical help in the process of expressing ideas on paper we thank Lt./Col. Glenn Wittbrodt of St. Louis, who teaches people how to write.

We thank Mrs. Muriel S. Karlin of Staten Island, New York, and Dr. William Crowder of Purdue University for many helpful suggestions for improvement of the original manuscript.

CONTENTS

CONTENTS

1

Identifying the Object
of the Teaching Game

It is a custom in our school to gather the teachers occasionally for a faculty bowling party. During one of these outings a well-muscled beginner, to both teaching and bowling, was teamed with a group in alley nine. While rolling in alley ten we had ample opportunity to watch the new teacher apply bushels of enthusiasm and raw energy to a frantic wind-up, a deft right-sway, a ferocious teeth-clenching, and a tight closing of both eyes as she released her ball through a high loft to bounce along the right gutter of her alley to the pit.

As the male half of this writing and bowling team prepared to exercise his slightly better form to the object of eliminating ten pins from alley ten, he paused to allow the new teacher to finish her roll in alley nine. Her frantic wind-up proceeded as usual, but this time the eye closing came before the right-sway. Following an unusually large right-sway she released her ball in a high curving arc over the alley nine gutter, and over the ball return trough. The ball crashed into the right gutter of our alley, climbed out of the gutter wobbling like a fifty-cent gyroscope, and proceeded down our alley for a perfect strike.

The girl delightedly cried out, "A strike!"

Obviously, the new teacher had not yet learned the object of the game.

In teaching, as in sports, it is impossible to win without first knowing the object of the game.

For school people the object of the game is learning on the part of pupils. The goal is learning evidenced by changes in a pupil's responses following instruction. Specifically, the goal can be learning evidenced by a pupil's reading of a word or passage that he could not read prior to instruction; or it may be learning evidenced by a pupil's solving of an equation that he was unable to solve prior to instruction. The goal may also be learning evidenced by the pupil's facial expression suggesting pleasure as he listens to a musical composition, when prior to instruction he responded to such stimulation with apathy or childish rejection. Or the goal may be learning evidenced by a student's eye contact, attentive countenance, and alert posture during teaching sessions, when prior to instruction the pupil did not appear to be paying attention during such sessions.

Working Definitions of Curriculum and Instruction

For purposes of clarity, the object of the teaching game is to move and/or aid pupils to do some desirable thing that they could not or would not do prior to instruction, so that following instruction they can and will do that desirable thing. The detailed plan for making desirable changes in pupil behavior is what is meant by *curriculum;* the activation of the plan to cause changes in pupil behavior is what is meant by *instruction.*

You know that in the real world this curriculum-instruction distinction is not so clear-cut as outlined above. Of course, curriculum and instruction are not discrete entities, but tend to run together at precisely the place where curriculum plans and materials are activated through instructional methods toward the object of changing the behavior of learners. Nevertheless, the terms *curriculum* and *instruction* as defined above, are useful in describing teaching activities, as the terms *directing* and *executing* are useful to describing corporation management activities.

Organizing the Job by Levels of Learning

Curriculum making and instruction giving, as defined above, comprise the activity of teaching. Teaching, as it is commonly understood, is complementary to and pointed toward learning. To lay out the job of teaching for examination and planning, it is necessary to describe learning in some way.

Modern educational psychologists have described the learning hierarchy in a number of different ways. For practical purposes, our purposes, it is helpful to consider four levels of learning. These are: familiarity, knowledge, understanding, and application. Once you grasp the four levels of learning concept to use when describing the object of the teaching game, you will find it easier to organize learning activities for pupils.

Familiarity is the lowest level of learning. If you began reading this book on page one, you now have a familiarity with its content. You know our definitions for three terms: teaching, curriculum, and instruction. You have some idea of what the book is about from reading the table of contents and the introduction. You could now carry on a low level discussion of what this book says. You are conversant with a part of what it contains. You are familiar with this book.

Knowledge is a slightly higher level of learning from familiarity. You have a knowledge of what you have read so far in this book. You can recall that a distinction has been made between curriculum and instruction, that the introduction promised an explanation of methods, and that the contents promise a discussion of Interaction Analysis. These are all facts that you can recall, given proper stimulation. The facts do not mean much at this juncture, but you (and the two of us) believe that as the facts are used throughout the book they will add up to something more.

The "something more" is the *understanding* level of learning. At the understanding level, facts from the knowledge level are put together to form conceptual discriminations and generalizations. These conceptual discriminations and generalizations do not constitute action, but they do form the basis and impetus for action.

The action takes place at the highest level of learning which is *application*. Your only reason for reading this book is to enable you to apply its suggestions to your own work with learners. The book was written for professionals who have reached the understanding and application levels of learning in the field of education. For this reason, you can move rapidly and easily to translate suggestions from this book to immediate practical action in your class or school. This translation of book learning into action is not possible with entry level books, such as are used in survey courses, since these books are intended only to build familiarity with, and knowledge of a certain field of study.

The levels of learning formulation is an important concept which will be utilized frequently in subsequent chapters. Table I has been prepared as a handy guide for future reference.

The modern algebra text will provide a familiar levels of learning example. Most texts begin with a discussion of uses of algebra in society, and this is followed by material designed to link the familiar mathematical expressions of reality to the unfamiliar algebraic expressions of reality.

Table I
LEVELS OF LEARNING

Level	Teacher Action to Build Level	Student Response at Level
Familiarity	Lecture, directed reading, or some expository technique designed to acquaint student with bare essentials of subject.	Student knows that subject field exists. Student has a very general idea of what the subject is about.
Knowledge	Lecture, directed reading, expository techniques, some discussions.	Student can recall isolated facts, can define most terms, and can make simple discriminations among concepts.
Understanding	Reading involving some student choice, teacher-student discussions, specific short lectures, project work, requirement for pupil to take positions and defend his positions.	Student has a conceptual understanding of the subject which is evidenced by his production of verbal and written remarks, and/or other activities. Student can discriminate among, and generalize from concepts within the subject field.

Level	Teacher Action to Build Level	Student Response at Level
Application	1. Motor Skills: Practice in doing the job under simulated or supervised real conditions. 2. Mental Skills: Utilization of understandings to solve problems or appreciate work of others.	Student can perform task well enough to enable him to function at the minimum acceptable level of beginners actually using the skill for work or recreation purposes.

This is an attempt by the text writer to develop the pupil's familiarity with the subject of algebra. Next comes a definition of sufficient terms or concepts to enable the pupil to perform a few simple transformation operations of whatever particular type the text author believes will help a beginner develop a knowledge level of algebra learning. The terms' definition is a move into the knowledge level of learning, and the pupil's practice work with the transformations is simply a pedantic device to aid the student in retaining his newly acquired knowledge. Subsequent pages in the algebra text engage the pupil in additional terms-memorization, transformations practice, and eventually simple translations of hypothetical real world situations to algebraic expressions. After the student has gained a knowledge of many definitions, transformations possibilities, translation techniques, and certain manipulative limitations, he is ready to see more elegant possibilities for translating moot situations to algebraic expressions, and for solving for unknown quantities in these expressions. This ability to put together the facts, definitions, and procedures of the subject is the understanding level of learning.

Finally, the pupil is directed by his text to draw upon his understanding of algebra to solve problems which can and do occur in the world outside of Algebra I. It is at this level of learning that the student applies his knowledge and understanding to solve real problems. He has reached the application level of learning.

You can use this concept of levels of learning to determine what you, or what other teachers, are asking of learners that is reasonable or unreasonable. Are you asking fifth grade children with third level reading skills to learn from fifth level social studies books? If so, you are demanding reading skill at the application level of learning from learners whose reading skills are at the knowledge level of learning. That does not work. Are you asking any of your tenth grade students who have difficulty discriminating between a complete and an incomplete sentence to write multi-paragraph themes? If so, you are demanding understanding level performance from learners at the familiarity level of learning. That does not work.

You can use the concept of levels of learning to correct the difficulties suggested above. First, discover where your pupils are in terms of their level of learning and the subject matter to be presented. Second, decide what makes sense in terms of the "next step" to move the pupils toward the application level of learning. If your pupils need familiarization, then they will respond with performance and progress (and decent deportment) to nothing else but familiarization activities. Or, do your pupils have a fair knowledge of the subject matter segment you are presenting? If so, move cautiously to bring this knowledge together to help the pupil reach the understanding level of learning.

Have your pupils a mastery of terms and concepts concerning the material you are presenting? Is this mastery broad enough to permit pupils to make the discriminations and generalizations necessary to apply their understanding to some independent use of a skill or appreciation? If so, then guide students to develop their understanding to the application level of learning. Move toward application by way of independent reading activities, independent writing activities, simulation exercises, full performance of the motor activity you have been teaching, independent exercise of the critical artistic sensitivity you have been working toward, or a supervised "solo" ride in the driver training car.

Practical Insights from Psychological Studies

Before moving to the business of putting into practice specific curriculum building and instruction facilitating procedures in your class or school, pause momentarily to examine six learning principles gleaned from the literature of educational psychology. The principles have been gathered from controlled observations of thousands of children. The principles come from both experimental and action research studies.

The first is the principle of readiness to learn. All professional educators are familiar with the principle of physiological readiness—the idea that we wait for the formation of sufficient physiological structures to enable a pupil to perform a task before we attempt to teach him to do some motor task such as throwing a football. No educator would try to teach an infant to write. The educator knows that the infant has not yet developed the visual discrimination, eye-hand coordination, small muscle control, or muscle strength to approach the task. No educator would criticize the puny boy in the industrial arts class for completing projects slowly. The boy does not yet have sufficient physical strength to allow him to manipulate hand tools without frequent rest periods. Physiological readiness is pretty obvious, but this is not true of psychological readiness.

Consider the child in your elementary school classroom who is continually demanding your attention. Or consider the seventeen year old girl who daydreams through your most brilliantly executed English classes. Or, if you have responsibility for managing in-service meetings, consider the teachers whose minds wander during your carefully prepared in-service meetings. Could it be that the elementary school boy is not psychologically ready to do anything but think about the nightly fights between his mother or dad? If so, he is not psychologically ready for learning. Possibly that seventeen year old girl is not daydreaming, but numbed by a fear that she is pregnant. Exercises in the use and appreciation of language appear insignificant when stacked against that problem. And the in-service meeting at three-thirty P. M. reaches teachers following a six hours plus day on the firing line, and just prior to the rush home to examine the day's production of practice work by pupils. It is amazing that some teachers do have the psychological readiness (and physical stamina) to learn from after school in-service meetings.

Teaching and learning are two sides of the same coin. The teaching—learning act requires effort on the part of both teacher and learner. If the learner is not physically and psychologically able to meet you to receive your educational offers, then your best teaching is wasted.

The demanding elementary school boy, the fearful high school girl, the exhausted teacher cannot simply be tossed on the educational scrap heap. Something needs to be done to make them psychologically ready to learn.

The "something" is the second learning principle, motivation. This is the same motivation of smiling countenance, teacher excitement, and hard sell reported in most teachers manuals. But it is also the recognition that the motivation techniques in the teachers manuals are for most pupils—those *ready* to learn—but not all pupils. There may be some days when the boy worried about parental fights will need to be occupied with some rote task, such as straightening your files, to get his mind away from his worries. Recognize this, and stop trying to force him to learn to compute in base five on those days. Real motivation toward making this child psychologically ready to learn can be supplied only by the guidance counselor, social worker, or a marriage counselor. Get help.

Worries about an unwanted pregnancy are stiff competition for Milton or Shakespeare. While the girl is worrying, we know of no way to motivate her desire to learn. As with the elementary school boy, she needs to be left alone with her concerns. It would be nice if a guidance counselor, friendly teacher, trusted administrator, or school nurse could gain her confidence and steer her to medical help to confirm or allay her fears. It would be nice, and it happens once in a while, but usually neither you nor anyone else discovers what the problem is or was in cases of deep adolescent fears.

The problem of the school principal, or manager of in-service programs is more easily solved. Hundreds of schools have found that a one-hour release time for in-service meetings provides a tremendous lift for teachers and puts them in the mood to participate in in-service learning.

Learner participation is the observable sign that the third learning principle has been followed. This is the principle of involvement. It is possible for learners to be physically and psychologically ready to learn, and for them to be motivated by a stellar hard sell by the teacher, yet these learners quickly lose their motivation as the lesson progresses. What happened? The learners were not involved in what took place following the motivation.

Involvement does not necessarily require observable physical activity on the part of learners. Clever lecturers retain their listeners' attention through a number of involvement techniqes discussed in Chapter 10. Clever discussion leaders keep all members of their discussion groups involved through similar techniques. The key to involvement is to first motivate physical or mental participation by learners, and then keep them participating throughout the lesson. In a way, involvement is on-going motivation.

The fourth learning principle was first stated by Thorndike as the *Law of Primacy*. Primacy, the state of being first, implies that what you teach first is retained best by your students. To recognize this principle is to recognize that if you introduce some fact, concept, principle, or skill incorrectly, it will be a most difficult task to "unteach" it later. This is not to imply that good teachers never make mistakes. It is simply a plea for careful planning, and a call to recognize that when "unteaching" is necessary, expect that it will be difficult.

The fifth principle was stated by Thorndike as the *Law of Exercise*. It is a recognition that human learners are not computers, that once is not enough if human learners are to remember something. Professional educators usually adhere to the principle of exercise when teaching mathematics, spelling, phonics, composition writing, and like subjects that lend themselves easily to repetition and exercise. The exercise principle is less remembered during attempts to teach intangible attitudes and skills involving deportment, classroom procedures, class government management, human relations, and certain social studies concepts. If you "must constantly tell them to stop talking," then maybe they have never been *taught* the type of behavior you require. The exercise principle is an essential part of that teaching.

The final learning principle is the principle of reinforcement. It is this principle that brings us back, full circle, to the principles of readiness and motivation. Reinforcement implies that the pupil will learn better and will respond positively to further instruction (be ready for and motivated toward) if his response to previous instruction was rewarded. The trick is to discover what is reward for a particular pupil.

For many pupils simply the satisfaction that comes from learning something new is sufficient reinforcement (reward) to make the learning permanent, and to motivate the pupils to desire more learning. Many pupils accept as reward the teacher's "very good, John" comment following a correct pupil response. Conversely, a neurotic child may translate a half-hour scolding by his teacher as a desirable thing, and immediately following the scolding go forth to repeat the act he was criticized for committing. Flexibility is your key to putting the principle of reinforcement into practice. If what you give as reward for learner behavior tends to please the child, does help him learn, and motivates him to persist in the behavior you want, then use it. If what you offer as reward is met with a wide yawn from your pupil, then try something else. Moreover, if a child persists in an undesirable behavior after you have punished him, try something else. What you define as punishment, he may define as reward.

A caution must be inserted concerning the use of punishment-type reinforcement. Punishment has never been shown to be effective as a reinforcement for attaining substantive (subject matter) learning goals. Indeed, it has clearly been shown to be a serious hindrance to helping pupils learn skills, intellectual processes, concepts, attitudes, and appreciations. The one exception to this nearly universally agreed upon caution is in the use of punishment type reinforcement to achieve managerial goals (proper deportment is one). Here, as stated above, negative reinforcement (punishment) seems to produce the desired behavior in some pupils when used with caution, and when the teacher finds a punishment device that is indeed undesirable to the child being punished.

Review What You Have Read

The object of this game of teaching, of building curriculums and actualizing them through instruction, is learning. It is possible to go through the motions of teaching without plan or object, just as it is possible to go through the motions of bowling without plan or object. However, neither activity so executed is of much worth.

The first step in clarifying the object of teaching is to organize the job at hand by levels of learning. The analysis of a specific teaching task to determine whether it is appropriate to work toward learner familiarity, learner knowledge, learner understanding, or learner application, and to then design activities to build the appropriate learning level is a prime method of clarifying a specific object of teaching.

The practical task of guiding learners to achieve familiarity, knowledge, understanding, or application is aided by your working understanding of six learning principles: readiness, motivation, involvement, primacy, exercise, and reinforcement. The six principles provide general guidelines underlying the specific suggestions for teaching practice found in this book. The six principles are aids to the attainment of the object of teaching.

2

Theories, Bridges, and Curricula

Teachers and Principals Should Make Curriculums

This entire chapter serves as an introduction to the following six chapters describing curriculum management. We hope this chapter will be helpful in providing an argument in favor of wide professional participation in curriculum making.

A growing body of literature on curriculum construction treats curriculum as an arcane art, described by complex theories and beyond practical value to practicing educators. We have constructed the argument which forms all of Chapter 2 to disabuse teachers of the notion that curriculum making is an arcane art, and to encourage practicing educators to take, or retain, control of their own curriculums.

The Chapter 2 argument begins with some historical background in the section titled, "Footnote." The historical report is necessary to a later part of the argument. The argument proceeds after the Footnote in four sections titled: "The Definitions," "The Setting," "The Argument," and "The Point."

Through this argument we hope to make clear that curriculum building is much more a matter of hard practical work than a matter of complex theorizing.

Footnote

It was necessary for the purposes of this chapter to mention the names of Houston Chamberlin and Bernhard Rust. These are not familiar names, and some explanation may be necessary.

29

Chamberlin was a British scholar who gained some following among German scholars during the late Victorian period. Chamberlin produced a work titled, *Foundations of the Nineteenth Century* which he represented as an anthropological-historical theory, and which was accepted as such, first by an influential group of German politicians, and later by most of a nation. The theory was ultimately used by the German Nazi party to legitimatize some of its members' forays into the business of "racial improvement." The theory also provided the Weimar Period German educators with a scholarly reason for supporting the Nazi political movement.

Rust was a provincial schoolmaster who got in on the ground floor of the Nazi movement in the early 1920's. In 1934, Rust became Minister of Science, Education and Popular Culture for the Third Reich. Rust's major contribution to Hitler's Germany was the production and implementation of a national curriculum for all Third Reich educational programs. Rust's guiding theory in this endeavor was Chamberlin's anthropological–historical theory.

I. THE DEFINITIONS

Theory

The term *theory* is presently used to include explanations of reality as basic as the structure of logic, and as ephemeral as the path from your house to our house. The term *theory* is presently used to include explanations of reality as general as the structure of matter, and as limited as one man's guess as to the location of his lost cuff links. The term *theory* is presently used to include explanations of reality as technologically useful as trigonometry, as productive of printed research as a theory of mammalian behavior, as thought provoking as a theory of electron motion, or as useless and as destructive as Huston Chamberlin's theory of Teutonic superiority.

These present uses of the term "theory" are lay uses. Scholars have considerably reduced the scope of the term to exclude from theory's label idle conversations about moving across a city, or searches for lost cuff links. This is not to suggest harmony among scholars in the use of the term. As with many things, the company of scholars changes its number in first direct, but later inverse proportion to the number of semantic limitations placed upon the use of the term, *theory*. For example, some scholars would accept this proportional relationship of semantic limitation and definition of *theory* as a theory. Happily, most would not.

Dr. Fred Kerlinger, of New York University, has been cited as a provider of an acceptable definition of theory for curriculum workers. According to Dr. Kerlinger:

> A theory is a set of interrelated constructs (concepts), definitions, and propositions that presents a systematic view of phenomena by specifying relations among variables with the purpose of explaining and predicting the phenomena.[1]

Bridge

The term *bridge* is presently used to include man-made structures designed to span spaces over which it is impractical to build roadways or walkways. Some educators may object to the "man made" part of this definition, but otherwise we present it as universally acceptable to scholar and layman alike.

Curriculum

The term *curriculum* is presently used to refer to something as basic as a written document, and to something as ephemeral as an unboundable, infinitely expanding happening. The term *curriculum* is presently used to describe a plan so general as to include the entire nation, and so limited as to describe a single exercise for a single child. The term *curriculum* has been as practically useful as the medieval alchemy, as stimulating to the production of printed material as our law courts, and as destructive as Bernhard Rust's dissemination of Chamberlin's notions..

These present uses of the term "curriculum" are made by both educators and the laity. In the publication *Contemporary Thought on Public School Curriculum*,[2] seventy-four leading curriculum workers produced fourteen different definitions of the term

---

[1] Kerlinger, Fred. *Foundations of Behavioral Research.* (New York: Holt, Rinehart and Winston; 1967.) p.11

[2] Edmund C. Short and George D. Marconnit (Eds). *Contemporary Thought on Public School Curriculum.* (Dubuque, Iowa: W. C. Brown Company; 1968.)

"curriculum." In the publication *Curriculum Theory*,[3] an additional seven definitions of the term were provided. To escape this deluge of definition, it is necessary to seek an historical argument to reach the high ground of acceptable terminology. Looking backward in time, there was once when the term *psychology* was in about the same confused state as the term *curriculum* is now.

In the early part of this century many psychologists engaged in great argument about the definition of psychology. Wundt had his definition, Titchner his, as did Angell, Freud, and the early Gestaltists. J. B. Watson finally produced a definition that is more or less accepted by scholars today:

> . . . that division of natural science which takes human behavior—the doings and sayings, both learned and unlearned, of people—as its subject matter.[4]

It is interesting to note that the Watson definition stilled (but by no means ended) the argument over the term "psychology" because of its simplicity, its emphasis upon the visible, and its avoidance of the emotion eliciting terms of the field and the time.

We submit that what Watson did for the term *psychology*, Beauchamp has done for the term *curriculum*. For Beauchamp:

> . . . a curriculum is a document containing an organized set of decisions about what shall be taught in a school, or a group of schools.[5]

A major building block in the argument presented in this chapter is the acceptance of Beauchamp's definition of curriculum. The defenses offered for the definition are the ancient defenses of parsimony, clarity, and simplicity.

II. THE SETTING

Theory

Philosophers of science visualize the relationships between modern sciences with an inverted pyramid representation such as

---

[3]George A. Beauchamp. *Curriculum Theory*. (Wilmette, Illinois: The Kagg Press; 1968.)

[4]J. B. Watson and W. McDougall, *The Battle of Behaviorism*. (New York: Norton Publishing Company; 1929.) p. 4.

[5]Beauchamp, *Curriculum Theory* p. 175.

found in Figure 2-1. The rationale for the diagram is that all sciences and their theories are related. Furthermore, some sciences by their nature underlie—form the base for—other sciences. The inverted pyramid rests upon the most basic of the sciences, logic. Logic and mathematics are the intellectual tools which form the base for, and lend structure to, all of the sciences. The empirical sciences differ from the tool sciences in that the empirical sciences accept as axioms certain physical observations.

The diagram shown in Figure 2-1 is an attempt to express a relationship among the various studies of nature and man. It is also a statement of an ordering for scientific explanation. The ordering is reductionist in the extreme. For example, the lowest level of empirical science, physical chemistry, deals with the most basic elements of matter. As one ascends the ladder in the pyramid toward the social sciences, the elements of study become larger and more complex. Interestingly, the theories also lose rigor. Recognizing this, many observers from the "hard" sciences argue that nothing in the pyramid above the level of biophysics could be classed as theory. For the purpose of this argument, we propose to defend that some psychologists, notably Pavlov, Freud, Hull and Wertheimer have expressed statements which satisfy Kerlinger's definition of theory.

Without a commitment to a position either that education is, or is not, one of the social sciences, or simply an engineering field, it is possible and perfectly reasonable to point-out that there is no such thing as a *theory* of education. Within Marx's diagrammatic representation of the sciences there is no theory above the level of psychology.

Bridge

There is no theory of bridge building.

Curriculum

In a survey of writings on the subject of curriculum, Short and Marconnit have represented statements by Goodlad, Saylor and Alexander, Fox, and Taba as curriculum theories.[6]

---

[6]Edmund C. Short and George D. Marconnit (Eds.). *Contemporary Thought on Public School Curriculum.* (Dubuque, Iowa: Wm. C. Brown; 1968.) pp. 217-219.

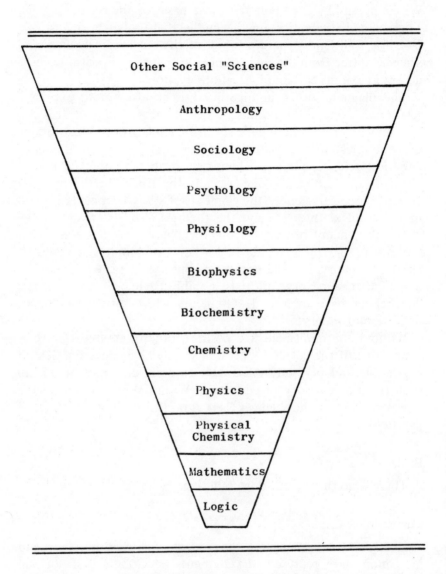

Figure 2-1. Pyramid of the Sciences.

In his paper, Goodlad mapped three levels of curriculum design.[7] Saylor and Alexander sketched four influences upon curriculum building in their paper.[8] Fox presented a simple explanation of gross aspects of curriculum planning in his work.[9] Taba has written a number of prescriptions for curriculum building and she has attempted to isolate certain curriculum elements. Not one of these statements provided a precise definition of terms, presented a systematic relationship among variables, or provided anything that made a testable contact with reality in terms of a verifiable proposition deduced from the body of the statement. Indeed, none of the five authors directly called his statement a theory, although Short and Marconnit represented them as such. Moreover, Goodlad, on one occasion wrote, "Curriculum theorizing to date is best described as abstract speculation. . . ."[10]

Beauchamp once suggested the existence of a curriculum theory in his article titled, "Curriculum Theory Applied to Urban Schools." In his article Beauchamp did provide some comment upon urban school curriculum building, but no theory.[11]

The applier of curriculum theory to urban schools, Beauchamp, later despaired:

> The curriculum theorist works toward the same general aims; he may use all of the procedures employed by any other theorist. The fact that curriculum theorists have not participated in all of these activities in the past may account for their failure to develop systematic curriculum theories up to the present time.[12]

The curriculum theory most difficult to dismiss is not even called a theory by its authors, although some curriculum workers

---

[7]John I. Goodlad. *Planning and Organizing for Teaching.* (Washington, D.C.: National Education Association; 1963.) pp. 19-22.

[8]J. Galen Saylor and William M. Alexander. *Curriculum Planning for Modern Schools.* (New York: Holt, Rinehart, and Winston; 1966.) p. 7

[9]Robert S. Fox. "The Sources of Curriculum Development," *Theory Into Practice.* 1:204, October, 1962.

[10]John I. Goodlad. "Curriculum: The State of the Field." *Review of Educational Research.* 30:195, June, 1960.

[11]George A. Beauchamp. "Curriculum Theory Applied to Urban Schools." in Short and Marconnit *Public School Curriculum,* pp. 224-229.

[12]George A. Beauchamp. *Curriculum Theory.* (Wilmette, Illinois; The Kagg Press; 1968.) p. 173.

have hailed it as "theory in the making." In 1967, Duncan and Frymier published what they called an "exploration in the systematic study of curriculum."[13] The study provided a number of definitions, and used these to relate constructs and propositions within a rigorous system constructed by Duncan and Frymier. In this way a systematic structure for viewing curriculum was detailed by the authors. The proposal suffered from a lack of contact with reality in that *individual learning acts* and *conceptual tracers* (defined terms within the Duncan-Frymier system) needed to be filled in with behavioral descriptions before a testable proposition could be generated from the system. Perhaps this is why Duncan and Frymier refrained from labeling their speculation as a theory.

There is no such thing as curriculum theory.

III. THE ARGUMENT

Theory

There is a necessity for arguing for the responsible use of the term *theory*. Without this necessity it would make little difference whether the scholar called his notion by the name notion, or preachment, or model, or theorette, or schematic, or theory. Indeed, the general public and Sir Arthur Conan Doyle have used the term *theory* as a synonym for *notion*. Why not the scholar?

Theories, so labeled by scholars, have a way of getting into the "woodwork" of society, and once there, on three occasions we can document, have caused a great deal of mischief. The first was the racist theory of Houston Chamberlin. It is impossible to prove that Chamberlin's theory was the cause or result of a prevalent attitude held by supporters of the Third Reich; nevertheless, Bernhard Rust got a great deal of help from Chamberlin in the way of legitimizing his curricular atrocities through appeal to Chamberlin's status as a theorizer.

As a second example, it is safe to state that the homeopathic theory of medicine died hard. Pasteur completed his classic work in bacteriology in 1881, and his ideas and practices had won wide

---

[13]James K. Duncan and Jack Frymier. "Explorations in the Systematic Study of Curriculum." *Theory Into Practice.* VI:180-189, October, 1967.

acceptance in Europe by the 1890's. Nevertheless, as late as 1915 one of Philadelphia's leading medical schools was still turning out homeopaths to go forth with hand picked herbs, gleaming scalpels, and mustard plasters to cure irritant with counter irritant. The mustard plasters are still with us, as is the notion that cold temperatures result in bacteriological and viral infections.

As a final example consider J. B. Watson's 1926 statement:

> Give me a dozen healthy infants, well formed, and my own specified world to bring them up in, and I'll guarantee to take any one at random and train him to become any type of specialist I might select—a doctor, lawyer, artist, merchant-chief and yes, even into a beggar man and thief regardless of his talents, penchants, tendencies, abilities, vocations, and race of his ancestors.[14]

Apparently the German scholars were not reading Watson during the thirties, for this rather flip statement from the platform of the creator of behaviorism initially influenced only U.S. society. Nevertheless, in spite of Watson's failure to make good his boast, in spite of the fact that behaviorism's real theoretical statement (Hull's) was shredded by research performed during the fifties, in spite of Bloom's[15] exhaustive survey of 1964, and in disregard of Jensen's[16] painfully careful study in 1969, the extreme environmentalist position presented by Watson in the guise of theory survives to this day to influence U.S. curriculums, public policy, and teacher guilt feelings.

Bridge

Bridge building is considered an engineering pursuit. The design engineer must bring to his craft theories of trigonometry and universal gravitation, and laws of aerodynamics, thermodynamics, metallurgy, meteorology, and geology. These disciplines are all utilized in the building of a bridge. There have been some unsound applications of aerodynamic and metallurgical principles in bridge

---

[14]John B. Watson. "Experimental Studies on the Growth of the Emotions." In C. Murchison (Ed.) *Psychologies of 1925*. (Worcester, Mass.: Clark University Press, 1926.) p. 10.

[15]Benjamin S. Bloom. *Stability and Change in Human Characteristics*. (New York: John Wiley and Sons; 1964.)

[16]Arthur R. Jensen. "How Much Can We Boost I.Q. and Scholastic Achievement?" *Harvard Educational Review*. 39:1-123, Winter, 1969.

building recently, and this has resulted in the collapse of a bridge or two. No one theorized as to why the bridges collapsed. Investigating engineers examined the wreckages and observed the causal faults. Once the faults were discovered, the technology was corrected.

Of course, bridge building involves more than engineering technology. A bridge project must be justified on the basis of need, financed, supported by a corporate structure to manage the people who will conceive it, design it, build it, maintain it, and use it. A scholar proposing a theory to explain the entire process would be laughed out of any structural design convocation in the world. Only bad technology is a problem in bridge building.

Curriculum

There are reasons for curriculum writers to be prudent with the stamp marked "theory."

Try to remember the heady world of 1962-64 when our nation was finally moving its haunches in preparation for a large infusion of wealth into academe for the betterment of society and education. It was at that time that social scientists and behavioral scientists were about to be given an opportunity to apply their theories to the building of the "Great Society." Why not? Theory, applied by scholars, had built the atomic bomb, conquered polio, produced penicillin and spacecraft. Why not, said the people, finance the social science theories. Head Start, Upward Bound, Higher Horizons, Community Action Centers, Job Corps, VISTA, the Teacher Corps, and projects resulting from a number of local and individual grants produced little. The reports describing these programs, constructed by men involved in the programs, were most discouraging.[17]

In addition to government agencies, teachers (both novitiates

---

[17]Donald Bourgeois. "The School in the Contemporary Community." Paper presented to the work conference of The Ohio State University Center for the Study of Curriculum. (The Ohio State University, Fall. 1968).

Thomas A. Billings. "Upward Bound Accomplishments." *Phi Delta Kappan.* October, 1968. pp. 95-98.

Daniel P. Moynihan. *Maximum Feasible Misunderstanding.* New York: Macmillan—The Free Press, 1969.)

U.S. Commission on Civil Rights. *Racial Isolation in the Public Schools.* (Washington, D.C.: U. S. Government Printing Office, 1967. Vol. I.)

and the initiated) have also assented to the preachments of blatant nonsense packaged under the "derived from theory" label, and postmarked with the name of a fashionable scholar. Bagley, high priest of John Dewey, sold an unsuspecting society a distorted progressivism in just this manner. Other "isms" are still being sold. Witness the fantastic current uses of the terms *learning theory*, *cognitive systems, curriculum theory, systems theory, games theory*, and even *individualization*. Possibly the freeing of teachers and administrators from the fear of violating the precepts of some theory they think they should practice, but somehow don't understand, would allow for more lively in-service discussion by the novitiate, and more honest trial and error in the classroom by the initiated.

Theory is desperately needed to explain and direct human learning. Thelen, Flanders, Cronbach, and Schwab have indicated the need for a theory of instruction. Use of theoreticians to pursue the less basic goal of curriculum theory tends to deprive talent from the pursuit of learning theory.

Teachers who represent their notions, and preachments, and technological systems as theories court loss of confidence from their colleagues in other disciplines, and from the public at large. Whyte in his charge of "scientism," Lynd in his *Quackery in the Public Schools*, and Hersey in *The Child Buyer* demonstrated this danger.[18] Swift, in another age, loosed a far more vicious attack upon misguided theoreticians than even his modern counterparts.[19]

IV. THE POINT

We view curriculum building as we view bridge building. Theory from many fields is needed for bridge building, but so are outside considerations separate from theory. Theory from many fields is

[18]William H. Whyte Jr. *The Organization Man.* (New York: Simon and Schuster; 1956.) Chapter 3.

Albert Lynd. *Quackery in the Public Schools.* (New York: Grosset and Dunlap; 1953.) Chapter 2.

John Hersey. *The Child Buyer.* (New York: The New American Library; 1962.)

[19]Jonathan Swift. *Gulliver's Travels.* (New York: Rinehart and Company; 1960.) Part III, Chapters 1-3.

needed for curriculum building, but so are other considerations outside of the realm of theory.

If, as we have predicted, educators soon settle for Beauchamp's definition of curriculum as a written document, then it should be easier for professionals to view curriculum building as a technological process to be mastered, like bridge building; and not as a natural phenomenon to be theorized about, like learning. If professionals accept Beauchamp's definition of curriculum as a written document, then suggestions for curriculum improvement such as this book contains will be seen as valid applications of technology to a technological problem, and not as indefensible theories to dazzle the gullible, and startle the initiated. Then curriculum argument can move from the futile debate of what should be taught, to the more fruitful laying of a philosophical groundwork to support decisions of what to choose from among the possibilities of what we know we can teach. Then professionals can look to their own good judgment for curriculum building guidance, and not be misled by a vague "curriculum theory." Then basic research and theoretical effort can be directed to the supporting disciplines of philosophy, sociology, psychology, political science, anthropology, and their sub-disciplines, leaving curriculum workers time to concentrate upon selecting from the disciplines, applications to the curriculum building functions of decision making, planning, personnel management, communication, evaluation, and the stipulation of specific learning goals. Then it will be recognized that attempts to build *the* curriculum theory are exercises in futility.

3

Developing a Realistic View
of Modern Curriculum

The argument in Chapter 2 identified curriculum as a plan; a written plan of what is to be learned by pupils, and when they are to learn it. In order to improve curriculum, to improve the overall plan for pupil learning, it is necessary to examine both the plan, and the forces which influence planning. Consider, for the next few pages, the following two points: what educators say curriculum is: and what curriculum really is.

The Way We Say It Is

Educators have always acted as if a thing called *curriculum* existed in their schools. Administrators make liberal mention of the high quality and technical beauty of the curriculum, their curriculum, in pompous speeches to parents and teachers alike. It is amazing that at some such speech a curious parent, or mischievous teacher has not interrupted the discourse, precisely at the time when the highest praise for The Curriculum was delivered, with the question, "What curriculum?"

Alas, it has never happened.

Because school people, usually public relations oriented school people, have never been called to give a detailed explanation of their curriculums, the public and some professionals really believe the popular notion that there exists in every school system a detailed plan outlining what each child should learn every hour of each day. This is evidenced by the panicky parents who send you notes asking that "make-up" work be provided for little Herkimer who yesterday missed thirty minutes of his social studies class for a dental exam. These parents really believe that Herkimer's total future progress in social studies is stalled until that missed thirty-minute learning segment is fitted into the puzzle that is Herkimer's mind.

Curriculum is a highly detailed, sequential plan for each minute of each school activity, that continues, in flow chart fashion, from kindergarten through grade twelve. That is the way we, or our spokesmen, say it is. Is curriculum really so rigidly set?

The Way It Is

There may be a school system somewhere which has a highly detailed, sequential plan for each minute of each school activity that continues in flow chart fashion from kindergarten through grade twelve. If such a school system exists, then it is a most unusual case, for such detail in curriculum definition is not "the way it is."

In our own studies of school system curriculum structures, we have identified three existing situations. You should be able to place your school in one of the three categories.

The Purchased Curriculum School

The most prevalent situation is the school system maintaining a dust covered State Curriculum Guide in each administrative office. The State Guide is usually supplemented by an equally unused local guide which, prepared or revised within the last ten years, was produced by a committee of teachers and administrators. The local curriculum guide adds little local embellishments to the state guide, and is used on only two occasions.

First, the local curriculum guide is used by speech making administrators as a security producing mental image to be summoned during times when "The Curriculum" is mentioned. Second, the local guide is given to new teachers who receive the document with favorable anticipation, read it with increasing skepticism, ask questions about it in bewilderment, and abandon it in favor of friendly personal guidance by an experienced teacher.

Furthermore, in this type of school, the local curriculum document is not considered when textbook selections are made. This omission tends to make the locally produced (and even the state department produced) curriculum ever less relevant to what is really being done in the classrooms. Textbook selections without matching the textbook to the previously written plan (curriculum) separates curriculum plan and classroom activities precisely because most modern textbooks are not just books, but are sequentially planned learning programs which teachers tend to follow. The new teacher, in particular, will use her "teacher's manual" for guidance in preference to the school's locally produced curriculum guide. She will do this because the teacher's manual is detailed, professionally written, and accompanied by printed and manipulative materials which are available without "scrounging" efforts on her part.

The Purchased Curriculum School can be summarized as one where curriculum is roughly defined by the textbook programs it adopts, and where curriculum changes with each new textbook adoption. In those subject fields where textbook programs are not used, individual teachers decide what will be taught and when, within the broad boundaries defined by how much local administrators know or care about what happens in classrooms.

The Exhausted Teacher School

A few school systems really do make an honest attempt to plan the overall learning content and sequence of their programs. These schools, like the Purchased Curriculum Schools, rely heavily upon commercial programs such as basal reading texts, or SRA kits, or PSSC programs, but they also attempt to merge these commercial curriculum segments into a detailed local plan. Furthermore, when decisions to purchase a new commercial program, or part of a program, conflict with the local curriculum, then the local curriculum document is changed to coincide with the program change.

Such schools are called "Exhausted Teacher Schools" because of the time demands upon teachers and administrators of first producing a well written, integrated thirteen-year curriculum plan; of next training teachers to follow the plan; and finally of supervising teachers to insure that the plan is being followed.

As an example of an Exhausted Teacher School, consider a

northern Ohio school studied by the authors. The school district provided one hour of released time for all teachers to work on producing a detailed local curriculum. Additional time needed for curriculum work was to be donated by the teachers, naturally.

The district teachers and administrators were a highly skilled and highly motivated group, most of whom desired a workable, detailed, practical curriculum plan that could and would be followed by classroom teachers in future years. They considered both plan and materials as they developed their school district curriculum.

As the curriculum building work progressed, the Wednesday afternoon meetings expanded from the initial 2:30 to 4:30 PM meeting, to later 2:30 to dinnertime meetings. Many committees soon discovered it necessary to break for dinner and return to meetings for a couple of evening hours of additional work. As the year progressed, and deadlines neared, planning committee members found that Wednesday meetings needed to be supplemented by long individual and small group work sessions on other days. Many teachers reported spending as much as ten hours per week in curriculum planning work in addition to their regular school duties. It should be obvious that this resulted in a seventy hour week for some of the more conscientious professionals. It should also be obvious that many of these teachers were exhausted by April when the project was completed.

During our second year of observation, the curriculum plan was put into operation. At first, teachers were delighted with having a concrete, though flexible, outline of the total school curriculum. They also liked being able to discover where their own programs fitted into the total school program. However, this delight soon faded when it was discovered that more after school meetings were required for teacher orientation and for planning adjustments to keep the curriculum realistic, and up-to-date as new commercial programs were added, or as difficulties were discovered in certain existing programs. By mid-year the interest of many teachers in further curriculum work began to flag, and resistance to further curriculum work became evident.

The final result was that curriculum adjustment meetings became less frequent, and the well conceived curriculum plan grew more and more unlike what was really happening in the classrooms as old programs were discarded, and new programs added.

The No Curriculum School

A few schools make no pretense, at least to the professionals, of having any planned curriculum at all. Teachers are expected to plan their own curriculums on the basis of their own values and judgment. This situation is most prevalent in certain high school courses such as sociology, psychology, advanced physical science courses and advanced math courses. Nevertheless, the curriculumless situation also exists in a few total school systems. For these systems, or curriculumless classes within systems, the administration expects that each teacher will produce a curriculum custom tailored to the needs of the children involved.

In one No Curriculum School, familiar to the authors, a sixth-grade teacher decided to do away with all planning for his classroom, and to simply hold a year long dialogue with his pupils. This teacher honestly valued the dialogue, and decided that dialogue would best serve his pupils' needs. The dialogue procedure greatly distressed the local administrators, and the teacher was eventually fired, but the dismissal procedure presented difficulties. It is nearly impossible to prove that a teacher is not doing what he is supposed to be doing, when school officials have not even roughly stipulated what is to be done. It should also be noted that the following year a curriculum guide was produced which changed the No Curriculum School to a Purchased Curriculum School.

Toward Accurate Curriculum Communication

The above discussion indicates that what our administrative officers communicate to the public about curriculum (what we say it is), and what curriculum really is are often two different things. Chapters 4 through 7 of this book provide steps to follow to erase the disparity between the published curriculum and what is being done in the schools.

Plan a Unified Program

It is necessary to fault certain Purchased Curriculum Schools and all No Curriculum Schools for an approach to education which invites one teacher's undoing what another teacher has done. It is conceivable under either the Purchased Curriculum or

No Curriculum condition for a high school pupil to get a Darwinian orientation in his third-period biology class and a Lamarckian orientation in his fifth-period sociology class. Similarly, it is possible in a Purchased Curriculum or No Curriculum school for a fifth-grade teacher to require pupils to utilize a Ginn diacritical marks system after the pupils have been carefully taught the Scott-Foresman diacritical system in grade four.

Overall school curriculum planning need not necessarily eliminate the presentation of different points of view to high school pupils, or the presentation of different symbol systems to elementary and middle school pupils. What overall school curriculum planning does is to alert teachers to these differences. Thus alerted, teachers can help pupils to evaluate points of view of symbol systems on their merits, and teachers can prevent pupils from rejecting the total school program simply because they sense contradiction.

Plan for Synergy

Related to the "doing-undoing" examples above is the loss of *synergy* which results from every teacher doing his own thing. Synergy is a concept from the marketing people which relates to conditioning aspects of learning. Synergy simply means the increased probability of learning resulting from a pupil's receiving identical information from many different sources.

The marketing industry's example of ultimate synergistic impact is the adman's dream of a man driving his car on a highway under the following conditions. As he drives, the man can see a brightly colored package of Wrigley's gum on his dashboard. The car radio is at that moment playing a Wrigley's jingle, while a billboard advertising Wrigley's gum is just coming into view. Just above the horizon the man can see a skywriter completing a Wrigley's message. Motivational psychologists would predict the driver's action will be to reach for a stick of Wrigley's gum. That's synergy.

Admen plan for synergy, and they have proved that a few multi-source messages have more influence upon human behavior than do many single-source messages. Educators, such as Louis Rubin of the University of California, teach that schools can also have increased influence upon pupil behavior through the application of synergistic principles to curriculum planning.[1]

Teachers, and preferably whole faculties, should plan for synergy. Attention to synergy in curriculum planning will provide opportunities for learners to exercise prior learnings. Additional exercise and reinforcement will both greatly increase the probability that initial learning will occur, and provide insurance that learners will retain what they have learned. In addition, synergistic presentations tend to increase the credibility of concepts, generalizations, attitudes, or procedures to which they are applied.

Practical Conclusions for Curriculum Builders

We have identified four reasons for curriculum planning. First, planning is necessary for adequate communications between school and public. Second, some type of realistic plan aids both teachers and administrators in carrying out their functions within the school, and it increases communications channels between them. Third, a master plan helps to prevent teachers from working, or appearing to work, at cross purposes, from "undoing" learning stimulated by other professionals. Finally, a curriculum plan can be constructed to exploit synergistic principles.

Once you have grasped these four objectives of sound curriculum planning, you are ready to move into the first step of curriculum building.

---

[1]Louis J. Rubin. "Synergetics and the School." *Teachers College Record.* November, 1966. 68:127-134.

4

How to Write
Curriculum Objectives

Imagine that you have just entrusted a builder with several thousands of your dollars so that he can buy materials to build your house. Suddenly, you observe the builder tearing up your architect's plan with the comment, "This plan will inhibit me. I'll be much more creative without it."

You would be upset.

Imagine that you have just boarded an airliner. As you take your seat you overhear the pilot instructing the stewardess to dispose of the flight plan and maps. "I feel too inflexible when I stay inside of those airways," he says. "Today I'm just going to fly."

You would leave.

A world famous writer once characterized creative work as ten percent inspiration and ninety percent perspiration. The writer went on to state that a good deal of the perspiration is expended in planning.

Good builders, pilots, and writers plan their work, and they would not dream of operating without plans. The work of successful corporate executives, marketing men, and other movers of our society is also characterized by extensive planning. Similarly, the work of highly successful teachers is also carefully planned.

This preface, this short *apologia* for planning, is necessary in a contemporary treatment of curriculum planning, for much nonsense has been written concerning objectless curriculums. When examined on face, the notion of an objectless curriculum, a plan without object, is as meaningless as a destination-less flight plan, or a building-less architectural plan. Objectives are the heart of the curriculum, and without objectives there can be no curriculum. It follows that the technical quality of the objectives contained in the curriculum go a long way toward determining the overall quality of the curriculum itself.

The Trouble with Objectives

Curriculum objectives are what many curriculum writers have told you teachers need, and what you have possibly said were not worth the time required for their preparation. You're right. Curriculum objectives, as they are commonly written, are too vague, or too pompous, or too unrealistic, or too flowery to do anything but grace the first page of a deservedly dust covered curriculum guide.

This discussion is not about educational objectives as they are commonly known. This discussion is about objectives that work for you.

Categorize Your Objectives

In this objectives-writing guide, curriculum objectives are divided into four categories. The first category involves straight-forward academic objectives which fit easily into the four levels of learning structure discussed in Chapter 1. The next three categories involve attitude-value objectives which most curriculum makers find difficult to deal with. It will be shown that the levels of learning structure can also be used to simplify the clear specification of the value objectives. A handy set of patterns for writing the four types of objectives is provided at the end of this chapter.

The objectives discussion in each of the four sections that follow will begin with an example of an unclear, non-working objective, and proceed to modify the objective until it becomes sufficiently specific to be a *working objective.*

I. ACADEMIC OBJECTIVES

Writing Working Academic Objectives

The academic objective describes the intended learnings from instruction designed to improve skills such as reading, writing, or arithmetic; technical aspects of the arts; technical aspects of language, literature, and sciences; and content material from the social studies. The first negative objectives example concerns the social studies. Consider this as an objective that does not work for anyone:

Pupils will gain facility in social studies.

Some curriculum objectives are that vague. What is needed first is a classification of the term "facility," and a system for making such a classification has already been discussed. Recall the Chapter 1 "levels of learning" discussion. The levels of learning classification provides four levels of "facility" which have meaning. Just which level of learning you should aim for depends upon your grade level, your children, and you. Whether you *should* aim to build *application,* or *understanding,* or *knowledge,* or *familiarity* in your pupils is a value decision specific to your estimate of what your pupils need to learn. How you state your curricular value decisions to provide clear direction for planning is a technological question treated here.

Consider the following change in the sample objective:

Pupils will gain a knowledge of social studies.

With the insertion of one defined term, *knowledge,* the objective has become more preposterous than before. Obviously, no pupil can possibly gain even a knowledge (ability to recall facts about) level of learning for all of the things called "social studies." Nevertheless, the insertion of the defined term "knowledge" has served to point up that the objective is too ambitious to be considered. In this way, a purpose has been served.

Further refinement of the objective requires a grade level designation. Seventh grade has arbitrarily been chosen for further example as a "mid-way" illustration for both elementary school and high school readers.

I. Social Studies—Grade Seven:
  A. Facts:
    1. Pupils will *know* (knowledge level):
      a. the capital city of each state in the U.S.
      b. the name and location of the following U.S. geographic features:
      (1) Mississippi River (Minnesota to the Gulf)

  (2) Rocky Mountains (Western U.S.)
  (3) Appalachian Mountains (Eastern U.S.)
  2. Concepts:
    1. Pupils will *understand* (understanding level):
      a. geographic and historic influences upon nineteenth century U.S. sectionalism
      b. the economic impetus for the U.S. population migrations of the 1850's, 1870's, 1930's, and 1950's
  3. Skills:
    1. Pupils will be able to *apply* map interpretation skills as follows (application level):
      a. can locate fifty U.S. state capitals on a U.S. map
      b. can measure distances between any two U.S. cities on a U.S. map

The outline is an example of how the levels of learning classification system is used to make working objectives. It is not intended as a model list of all seventh grade social studies objectives, or even as a complete list within categories. Such an outline, greatly expanded, does tell the teacher precisely what pupils are to learn.

Such specificity of objectives is easy to achieve for the social studies learning selected for the example. This is equally true for objectives in subjects even less value-laden than the social studies, such as most learnings in language arts (English and foreign), mathematics, sciences, home economics, business, and technical education courses. The problem that is always raised when specific objectives delineation is at issue is the subject of attitudes and values. No treatment of objectives determination is complete until this problem has been treated.

II. VALUE OBJECTIVES

1. Appreciation of Sensual Beauty

There is a story of two men viewing the Grand Canyon for the first time. One man stood for hours at the lip of the canyon languishing in the beauty of the play of sunlight and shadow on the canyon walls. After drinking deeply of the awesome beauty of the canyon spectacle he was just preparing to leave when a second visitor rushed to the same vantage point, took in the scene at a glance, and rushed away exclaiming, "Wow! That's some ditch!"

Who *appreciated?* Who valued the experience? Both men did in their own way.

The impatient man who captured the "big ditch" in a glance, and fled, was obviously more impressed by bulk than by beauty. The patient man who presumably drank deeply of the subtle beauty of the canyon spectacle was more impressed by beauty than by bulk. The two men appreciated the experience in different ways.

Would you praise the hurrier for appreciating only the gross feature of size in the Grand Canyon experience? Or would you praise the other man for indulging in a presumably sensual appreciation of the play of changing sunlight on the canyon walls?

Of course your answer to the question of which man to praise depends upon your own values, the things *you* appreciate. The answer is specific to the person giving the answer. The curriculum maker can insist that all pupils move to *know* the capital cities of all U.S. states; but the curriculum maker cannot insist that all pupils appreciate the beauty of the architecture of the capitol buildings in those cities *in the same way the curriculum builder appreciates them.* One thing that any teacher can aim to do is to *familiarize* (provide exposure to) pupils with some beautiful experience, and allow them to appreciate the experience in their own way. Without a knowledge of the teacher's values then, an "appreciation of sensual beauty" objective should be changed from the usual overly ambitious statement:

Pupils will appreciate the music of Beethoven.

to the more modest, yet attainable objective:

I. Pupils will be familiar with the following works by Beethoven (familiarity level):
A. *Concerto in D Minor*
B. *Symphony Number Five*
C. *Moonlight Sonata*

The above objective is the best that can be achieved unless some assumptions concerning who is going to do the teaching are made. If the teacher is indifferent to Beethoven's work, or if the teacher frankly dislikes Beethoven's work, then the objective, as corrected above, is best left as it is. The reasoning behind this prescription is that the teacher who does not himself experience a feeling of sensual stimulation and pleasure in the presence of a *specific* sensual experience cannot infect others with such an emotional reaction. In this teacher's classroom the experience will need to stand or fall on its own merits.

On the other hand, assume that a teacher is truly incapable of sensual indifference to certain renditions of specific Beethoven compositions. Then it is possible for this teacher to infect at least some pupils with a similar tendency to gain sensual pleasure from experiencing certain of Beethoven's works. The teacher with a true appreciation of certain experiences purported to represent beauty can present to pupils: (1) experiences containing the beauty; (2) the experience of observing the teacher appreciating the beauty; and (3) the teacher communicating his appreciation. For this teacher the objective should read:

I. Pupils will gain an *understanding* of the following works by Beethoven so that pupils are equipped to appreciate them (understanding level):
   A. *Concerto in D Minor*
   B. *Symphony Number Five*
   C. *Moonlight Sonata*

Raising the learning level from *familiarity* to *understanding,* and adding the phrase "equipped to appreciate" prescribes a greater exposure of pupils to both the objective-specified musical compositions, and to the teacher who loves the compositions. The ultimate goal of true appreciation of sensual beauty and tendency to experience sensual pleasure from future exposure to Beethoven is not stated. It is not stated because the intangible goals of appreciation and pleasure cannot be guaranteed by any curriculum or instructor. The best the curriculum plan can state as proper aim in the area of sensual beauty objectives is the setting of conditions so that teacher to pupil contagion of teacher preferences is likely.

Objectives writing in the area of sensual appreciation must consider both the preferences of the teacher, and the ephemeral process through which people acquire preferences for certain· sensual pleasures. Curriculums which ask teachers to fake preferences for sensual appreciations are doomed to failure; so are curriculums which assume that all pupils can be taught to love the arts in the same manner that they are taught the multiplication tables.

2. Acceptance of Philosophical, Ethical, or Political Values

Separate from the acquisition of appreciations of sensual beauty are pupils' acceptance of certain philosophical, ethical, or political values. One commonly seen objective in the political-philosophical category reads:

Pupils will appreciate the values of democratic living.

The objective has a satisfying ring to it, and it is particularly comforting to officers of State Departments of Education, or legislators—anyone who both values the democratic political system, and knows nothing of teaching children. The problem with the political-philosophical objective given as example is that it leaves the total definition of what constitutes "democratic living" up to the reader.

Curriculum writers need to define the components of objectives such as "democratic living," or "good citizenship," or "social conscience," or "respect for others." As an example, observe how the objective below rephrases the "democratic living" example to gain specific direction for the teacher:

I. Pupils will evidence the following *voluntary* applications of democratic principles (application level):
   A. participation in student council activities
   B. use of democratic devices in school activities:
      1. petitions   4. constitutions and by-laws
      2. votes   5. student political parties
      3. rational debate
   C. participation as "loyal opposition" when part of a minority school political group

It should be obvious that a good deal of familiarity, knowledge, and understanding of democratic political process must be built before pupils are able to make the applications demanded in the objective. That is part of what objectives are for—to let the teacher know what needs to be done in order to successfully reach the objective specified in the curriculum. Working objectives do this, while the usual objectives just sit on the page looking pretty.

The sample "democracy" objective also has a voluntary aspect. Any objective that deals with values must have a voluntary aspect, for when a person truly holds a value he will not act contrary to it. If your pupils are extolling the virtues of democracy in sociology class, and organizing themselves into dictator directed motorcycle gangs after school, they do not value democracy. A student writing a decent paper in praise of democracy while the student is at the same time voluntarily participating in an after-school two-bit dictatorship indicates only that the student has learned to play the familiar game of "humor the teacher."

3. Acceptance of Other Values

Many values that schools are charged with teaching do not fall easily within the categories of Sensual Beauty Appreciation, or Philosophical-Ethical-Political Values. These "other values" tend to change with the times, with geographic locations, or with special circumstances within certain communities. Examples of these "other values" are preferences for certain diets, acceptance of certain medical or hygenic regimens, and avoidance of certain activities considered harmful by the community. An example familiar to all elementary school teachers is the taboo against young children accepting auto rides offered by strangers. This situation will make a good example for further development of the "working objectives" technique. No one would write the negative example as it is below, yet it is no worse than previously given negative examples:

Children will fear and mistrust all strangers.

Certainly you do not want to teach children to fear and mistrust all strangers; you simply want them to move to and from school by safe and predictable means. Specific, working objectives tend to avoid the ominous overtones of the "fear and mistrust" objective. Be specific and say:

I. Children will *understand* the necessity for politely avoiding contact with strangers.

II. Children will *voluntarily* avoid contact with strangers.

To determine whether or not objective *I* has been reached you would simply ask a child to react to a hypothetical stranger, and to explain his reaction to you.

The attainment of objective II will be evidenced when children report to you how they avoided a stranger who tried to entice them into his car, or offered to "treat" them in the local candy store. Hopefully, it will also be evidenced by zero cases of children in your school being abused by child molesters.

What Working Objectives Do for You

There are seven benefits that you as curriculum builder reap when you use objectives that work for you. These are:

1. The size of the teaching job is indicated.
2. A guide to the organization of learning activities is provided.
3. A specification of cognitive learning or value learning is made.
4. A precise specification of what is to be learned is available.
5. Ultimate value objectives are assigned a necessary "voluntary aspect."
6. Overgeneralization of objectives to include unintended and/or undesirable learnings is prevented.
7. Testable ultimate ends are available.

Guidelines for Writing Working Objectives

Three general principles govern the writing of working objectives. These are:

1. Classify your objective as academic, value-sensual beauty, value-philosophical, value-ethical, or value-other.
2. Decide the level of learning you need to attain and specify it in your objective.
3. Clearly state the ideal behavior expected of learners after the objective has been achieved.

Patterns for Writing Working Objectives

Some of the concepts for writing working objectives presented in the previous discussion are complex, and professionals wishing to make use of the concepts may desire further guidance, beyond the "example" treatment, for writing their own objectives. For this reason, there follows a section giving patterns for writing curricular objectives in the "working objectives" form. These patterns are rules of thumb intended to aid, not limit, the objectives writer.

Each pattern gives a manuscript print "skeleton" which has been filled-in with cursive print specifics. Try using the manuscript skeleton to form your own objectives to the "working objectives" pattern. The final line within subcategories of each pattern has been left blank for this purpose. The construction of "working objectives" is not an art, it is a habit. Filling-in the final line will help you to acquire the habit.

The remainder of this chapter is divided into five patterns: two patterns for writing academic learning objectives; a pattern for writing appreciation of sensual beauty value objectives; a pattern for writing philosophical-ethical-political value objectives; and a pattern for writing other value objectives.

Pattern for Writing Academic Learning

Objectives – Pattern I.

Subject: _Language Arts_   Grade: _three_

   I.   Facts: Pupils will know:

       A.   the _twenty-six letters of the alphabet in_

             order

       B.   that _the dictionary is used to find the_

             meaning of words

       C.   that _____
             (anything of a purely factual nature)

II. Concepts – pupils will understand:

       A.   that _at times many attempts must be made to locate_

             the proper spelling of a word

       B.   that _the dictionary organization is based upon an_

             alphabetical order system keyed to the first letter

             of a word

C. that *the dictionary organization is based upon an alphabetical order system which operates from left to right to decide order among words with identical beginning letters*

D. that _____
(any understanding)

III. Skills - pupils will be able to apply *dictionary skills* as follows *(Scott Foresman Beginning Dictionary):*

    A. can locate *words for which spelling is provided by the teacher*

    B. can locate *words pronounced by the teacher*

    C. can use *the pronunciation guide to determine the sound of phonemes:*
        1. *controlled by short vowels*
        2. *controlled by long vowels*

    D. can _____ to
(any active verb)

_____
(any observable act)

Pattern For Writing Academic Learning Objectives
Pattern II

Subject: *Algebra*   Grade: *nine*

V. *Unit Five - operating with monomials*

    A. Pupils will be familiar with *uses of:*
        1. *monomial addition and subtraction to simplify expressions*
        2. *monomial multiplication and division to simplify expressions*

B. Facts - pupils will know:

    1. *the definition of "term"*
        _____

    2.
        _____
                (any technical definition)

C. Concepts - pupils will understand:

    1. the *application of the distributive property of*
        multiplication to the addition of monomials

    2. the use of *commutative and associative*
        properties of number in the multiplication of
        monomials

    3. the _____
                (other relationships)

D. Skills- pupils will be able to:

    1. *simplify monomial addition examples such as:*

        a. $2x + 3x$ b. $-4x + 5x$

        c. $-6x + (-7x)$ d. $-5x + 4x$

Pattern for Writing Sensual Beauty Objectives

Pattern III

Subject: *Art Appreciation*   Grades: *ten - twelve*

Teacher: *Mr. Arte*   (appreciates works below).

 I. Pupils will be familiar with:

    A. *Metropolitan Museum Reproductions of:*

        1. *"Self Portrait" by Van Gogh*

        2. *"Arrangement in Grey and Black" by Whistler*

        3. _____
                (other specific reproduction)

    B. *locally available originals*

        1. _____
                (list specific works)

II. Pupils will gain an understanding of the following works of art so that they are equipped to appreciate them:

A.   _"The Last Supper" by Dali_

    1.   _use of contemporary color in classic work_

    2.   _meanings of symbols_

        a.   _sunset_

        b.   _duodecagon_

        c.   _pathway_

B.   _____
        (other works appreciated by teacher)

    1.   _____
            (specific features for study)

Pattern for Philosophical-Ethical-Political
Value Objectives – Pattern IV.

Grade or School Level: _five_

Subject: _social studies_

I. Honesty:

  A. Pupils will know:

    1.   _Hammarabi's prescription for honest behavior_

    2.   _the eighth commandment of Moses_

    3.   _____
            (other ethical pronouncement)

  B. Pupils will understand:

    1. logic of _Christian "Golden Rule"_

    2. function of _local laws prohibiting dishonest acts_

    3.   _____
            (other arguments for honest acts)

C. Pupils will voluntarily (application):

1. _return lost articles of value to the_
   school office

2. _correct the lunchroom cashier when she gives_
   excessive change

3. _refrain from using "ponies" while writing_
   examinations

4. _____
   (other examples of voluntary behavior)

Pattern for "Other Values" Objectives

Pattern V

Subject: ___Health___   Grade: ___seven___

I. Cigarette Smoking (subject will be presented by a teacher who is a non-smoker):

A. pupils will know:

1. that   _cigarette smoking increases incidence of:_
   a.   _heart disease_
   b.   _lung cancer_

2. that   _cigarette smoking causes:_
   a.   _bad breath_
   b.   _emphysema_

3. that _____
           (other related knowledge)

B. pupils will understand:

1. distinction between   _physiological and_
   psychological dependence

2. how   _medical researchers have related cigarette_
   use and disease
   a.   _Stanford University Human Research Study_
   b.   _Harvard "rat studies"_

3. _____
           (other relationships)

C. pupils will voluntarily:

   1. report   *intention to refrain from smoking*
   _____

   2. _____
                          (other relevant behaviors)

Objectives Overview

This chapter has presented a method for writing working curriculum objectives. The four levels of learning concept was utilized to direct objectives construction. The objectives writing patterns described are patterns for writing curriculum plan objectives at the grade, grade level, department, or school level. The patterns are too broad for specific daily lesson plans, and too narrow for an ultimate kindergarten through grade twelve school district plan. Chapters 5 and 6 describe a system for constructing ultimate school district objectives, and for fitting the grade, grade level, department, and school level objectives into a total curriculum plan.

5

Making the Curriculum Pieces
Fit Together

Our aged Aunt Anna is a devotee to the activity of assembling picture puzzles. She has advised us that the most challenging puzzles are those which make no picture at all, but instead result in an intricate, near chaotic, design of curved lines and complex patterns. Moreover, this proficient puzzle-piece fitter assures us that there is an ultimate challenge to picture puzzle masters such as herself. The ultimate challenge is to attempt to assemble the toughest of pattern puzzles without once referring to the big picture printed on the puzzle box lid. We cite Aunt Anna as a leading expert in picture puzzling, and accept her counsel for achieving maximum challenge from assembling picture puzzles.

If the various learning tasks carried on in a kindergarten through grade twelve school are viewed, metaphorically, as pieces of a pitcure puzzle, then it follows that assembling the educational tasks into a coherent curriculum is made easier when curriculum builders have a "big picture" as a guide. Unlike Aunt Anna, educators are not interested in increasing the difficulty of their task, but are intensely interested in attaining an effective finished product. Unfortunately, the educator does not get a "picture" with his curricular puzzle pieces; he only gets the pieces.

Fitting Curriculum Pieces

"Big pictures" need to be constructed for each level of educational effort—single classroom, single grade or subject, total department or total school, and total school system. The "big picture" construction can be initiated at any of these levels of educational effort, and thus can provide curriculum guidance for a single classroom, a group of classrooms, a single school, or a total school system.

Ideally, the "big picture" construction is initiated by the school superintendent, and provides guidance for curriculum construction through all levels of the school system. That is the ideal.

Few educators work in ideal situations, and few superintendents read books on curriculum. Therefore, the curriculum discussion in this chapter has been inverted from the usual "top-down" theoretical discussion, and it begins with positive steps that the individual teacher, working in isolation from other teachers and administrators, can take to construct his own "big picture."

Fitting Curriculum Within the Classroom

The elementary school teacher working in a self-contained organization, the secondary teacher working in a separate subjects context are both curriculum lords in their own castles. Within, at worst, undefined boundaries, or at best, unbelievably broad boundaries set by State Departments of Education or local tradition, teachers so situated choose between drifting aimlessly from topic to topic as the day's mood directs, or following a plan of their own making. Those who choose to plan must make their own plans. Here's how to begin.

First, define your ultimate goals for the year. What can you reasonably hope to achieve at the termination of *your* work with children next June? Begin by dismissing from your mind superficial goals such as preparing children for the next elementary grade, or preparing pupils in this year's general biology for advanced biology next year. It has already been assumed that you do not even speak to other teachers in the school, let alone plan with them. The question is, what can you reasonably expect your pupils to achieve this year?

Consider your materials. Ideally, you plan your curriculum and then order materials to suit the plan. Fine idea. Do that if you are sufficiently wealthy to buy the materials you need. Otherwise, you had better plan to work with essentially the materials supplied by your employer.

What textbooks do you have? What goals do these texts strive for? Most modern textbooks list, at least in the teacher's manual, rather specific objectives for day to day lessons as well as broad objectives for the entire text-program. These text objectives listings give a most helpful start; for whenever you agree with an objective of the text writer you can lift the objective whole from the text writer's program as your own.

Classify the text objectives that you accept, first according to subject matter (elementary) or unit (elementary or secondary) headings. Consider a listing from an intermediate grade English program as example:

OBJECTIVES: English; Grade 5

1. Improve pupil oral expression in:
   a. classroom reporting
   b. formal discussion
   c. social situations
2. Develop pupil ability to recognize eight parts of speech:
   a. noun   e. preposition
   b. pronoun   f. adverb
   c. verb   g. article
   d. adjective   h. conjuction
3. Develop pupil ability to:
   a. discriminate between a complete sentence and a phrase
   b. write a complete sentence
4. Develop pupil ability to utilize effective paragraphing techniques.
5. Improve pupil use of writing conventions:
   a. punctuation:
      (1) end punctuation   (3) comma parenthetical
      (2) comma pause   (4) comma series
   b. capitalization
6. Build appreciation of poetry.

The sample objectives could be found in almost any intermediate grade English text teacher's manual, and the vague (by the standards of the preceding chapter) language in objectives statement is not uncommon. However, a simple listing, such as the above, does provide you with a "big picture" view of your year's English program. Look at it.

The next step is to decide what makes sense for your pupils. The text assumes an "average" English achievement level on the part of pupils. The text also assumes that the pupils' application level reading ability is about one level below the grade level designation of the text. Have most of the pupils in your class reached a level of achievement in English which indicates that the material suggested in the text listing is a logical "next step" in their development? Have most of the pupils in your class achieved an application-level reading ability of at least one grade level below their present grade level placement?

If the answer to either or both of the questions is "no," than you are ill advised to utilize the text as it is intended to be used by the publisher. In this event you have three choices: (1) submit requisitions to your principal until he buys you materials that you can use; (2) write your own program; or (3) adapt the program that you have to fit the needs of your pupils. The third possibility usually works, except in extreme cases. The first possibility (requisition of new materials) will save a great deal of adapting effort, but depends for success upon both the principal's understanding of sensible curriculum practices and the size of his budget.

The second possibility (write your own) is not recommended for elementary school teachers in academic areas such as English. The elementary teacher *must* write some programs in areas such as group guidance and physical education; therefore, it is unwise to use valuable teacher time to write programs in subject areas where nearly every conceivable program already exists.

The secondary school teacher sometimes does have both the need and the time to write complete programs for his own specialty. Whether or not the secondary teacher writes his own programs is dependent upon the number of preparation periods allotted the teacher, the number of different subject assignments given the teacher, and the availability of suitable text-program materials.

For example, the secondary teacher meeting six periods per day of two math, two physical science, and two biological science classes does not have time to read the texts he is using let alone write his own programs. Moreover, it would make little sense for the teacher of an average ninth-grade math group to write his own algebra program. There are so many commercial programs to choose from it is difficult to imagine a teacher so demanding that he could not at least adapt an existing program or programs to his needs and the needs of his pupils. On the other hand, the secondary teacher of sociology assigned to meet four sociology classes per day has both the time, and the need to develop his own sociology programs. A commercial sociology program suited to his pupil's needs may not exist.

Returning to the intermediate-grade English example, recall that the teacher is making a decision of what to include in his "big picture," his year's objectives. Assuming the text objectives can be accomplished, the next question is should they be accomplished? In most text-programs the program contains more material than can reasonably be used in a single-year program. Publishers admit this, in fact, they consider it a strong point in their programs. The excess of material over time provides whoever is directing curriculum with a choice among a number of worthwhile activities. What you choose is a value decision which a book cannot make for you. The only prescription on this point is that in the absence of deliberate teacher choice, the teacher will run out of time approximately three chapters before he runs out of program. In that event, the choice of what to exclude is made by the calendar, and this is indefensible pedagogy.

Avoid indefensible pedagogy. List your major objectives (self-made or from a program). Decide whether or not the objectives make sense for the achievement level of your pupils. Decide whether or not the objectives make sense in terms of your values, and the values of the community in which you teach. Decide whether or not you can reasonably bring most of your pupils to meet the objectives within your allotted quarter, semester, or year. Use professional judgment to eliminate certain objectives should you decide time is too short to achieve all objectives.

The preceding paragraph was a summary of all of the prescriptions for adapting particular commercial program objectives to your specific situation. The listing of text objectives should take no more than five minutes per text or program. Remember, concentrate upon major objectives, the "big picture." The rest of the steps involve decision making, and how much time this consumes depends upon your personality. Most important, you cannot yet complain that all of this takes too much time. Actually, this explanation is consuming more time than you will need to make the suggested objectives listing.

The objectives listing itself is valuable, and it has already served a purpose. It has helped you to decide whether or not the text-program is useful for your class, it has helped you to decide which objectives of the text-program to eliminate, it may have guided you to modify certain objectives, or to merge the objectives from two or more programs to yield what you desire. All of this for only five minutes per subject worth of list making, and from ten minutes to one hour of decision making. Some teachers do less, but some do more.

For the some who do more those intermediate-grade English objectives, or any general list copied from a text-program will need to be expanded and altered. The objectives will need to be altered to fit the four levels of learning format for "working objectives" discussed in Chapter Four.

An example will be provided utilizing objectives number three and six from the intermediate grade English objectives. Remember that these read:

3. Develop pupil ability to:
   a. discriminate between a complete sentence and a phrase
   b. write a complete sentence

Neither objectives listing is specific enough to provide sufficient teacher guidance for practical action. Objectives 3a and 3b are clearly academic objectives, and can be stated in the form suggested by the Chapter Four pattern.

III. Sentence Writing:

    A. Pupils will be familiar with:

        1. *examples of complete and incomplete sentences*

        2. *examples of incomplete sentences represented as complete sentences*

    B. Pupils will know: *the teacher's (or text writer's) definition of a sentence*

C. Pupils will understand:

1. *the difference between the subject and predicate in a simple declarative sentence*

2. *that a declarative sentence may be presented on the pattern:*

    a. *subject-predicate*

    b. *predicate-subject*

3. *the difference between the subject and predicate in a simple interrogative sentence*

4. *that an interrogative sentence is often presented in the pattern, predicate-subject-predicate*

5. *that the subject-predicate concept is a useful aid to testing sentences for completeness*

D. Pupils will be able to (application):

1. *label a group of complete or incomplete sentences as complete or incomplete declarative sentences*

2. *label a list of incomplete declarative sentences as missing either subject or predicate*

3. *write a complete, simple declarative sentence*

4. *write a complete interrogative sentence*

Objective number six can be stated according to the "Pattern for Writing Sensual Beauty Objectives." As you read the example for objective number six, assume that the teacher using the objective has a love and appreciation for the works to be presented. Without this assumption, the objective would simply prescribe pupil "familiarity" with a number of listed poems.

VI. Poetry

    A. **Pupils will be familiar with:**

        1. *Sir Patrick Spense*

        2. *The Unknown Citizen by W. H. Auden*

    B. **Pupils will gain an understanding of the following works so that they are equipped to appreciate them:**

        1. *Sir Patrick Spense*

            a. *statement of the omnipotence of medieval kings*

            b. *conflict between Spense's knowledge of the sea, and his fear of disobeying the king*

            c. *convention of mentioning the first-quarter moon as an ill-omen*

        2. *The Unknown Citizen by W. H. Auden*

            a. *the significance of the citizen's number in the dedication*

            b. *avoidance of direct reference to the citizen*

c. _use of listing of tangible possessions_
    as the indicator of the citizen's
    worth

d. _use of sharply clipped statements_
    suggest official detachment from human
    considerations

Assuming that the above, restated objectives have been taken from an available text-program, the daily lesson objectives and exercises pointed toward meeting the objectives are already in the program. Therefore, the teacher can proceed to work toward the objectives by simply following the text-program. The reason for listing the objectives was to provide the teacher with a "big picture" of the curriculum segment to enable him to eliminate inappropriate materials, and to add materials to strengthen the program. The restatement of remaining vague objectives to the "working objectives" format was prescribed so that the teacher could obtain a clearer "big picture" to provide daily lesson direction as the program is implemented.

Remember, it was stated that a simple listing of objectives, as they exist in the text-program, takes but little effort, and is a positive step toward making necessary selections from among instructional possibilities.

The second step, translating from vague objectives statements to working objectives statements, is more time consuming, but worthwhile in providing a clear "big picture" for instructional efforts direction. If you decide to put forth the additional effort required by the objectives translation, the third and final step, pacing, is easy.

To get an estimate of the pace of the program, simply note a date estimate beside each major objective heading. For example:

VI. Poetry: _March 15th to March 19th_

Making informal estimates of how the program will progress will aid in:

1. informed advance ordering or gathering of supplementary materials such as film strips or models.
2. keeping you up-to-date on whether or not you can reasonably expect to complete the planned program.
3. providing an indication that you need to add educational experiences to the plan when ahead of estimate, or make additional elimination decisions when behind the estimate.
4. providing elementary and middle school professionals with a timed, comparable listing of all objectives for all subjects. Such a listing will indicate overlaps between English, reading, and spelling; between any of the language arts and social studies; or between science and math. These overlaps may suggest curriculum fusion in some instances, different timing or presentation in other instances. Overlaps can also be magnified to obtain planned curriculum synergy.

Review Classroom Curriculum Fitting

This chapter has detailed five steps you can take in any classroom to create a practical curriculum. The plan does not require additional money, and requires little time for execution. The five steps to aid teachers in personal curriculum organization can be summarized as:

1. Organize your curriculum plan with reference to instructional materials you now possess or can get quickly.
2. Make a skeleton plan of broad topics to be treated for one year. Do this for each subject you teach.
3. Examine your plan for applicability to the achievement levels of your pupils.
4. Revise your plan (add or drop material) to fit both the achievement levels of pupils, and the time limitations of the school year.
5. Refine the major objectives in your plan to fit the "working objectives" classification scheme, levels of learning scheme, and behavioral statement formats.

The above five steps are steps you can take toward fitting together a rational curriculum. There is no requirement for an all district, all school, or even all grade level, team, or department effort to make the plan work, Neither is there a requirement for extra money to buy additional materials. All that you need to activate the plan is your desire to have for yourself a professional, rational curriculum plan. Make that decision, and you are on your way.

Beyond Classroom Curriculum Fitting

Many professionals are coming to realize that old "every teacher a king in his classroom castle" concept is not an ideal for which to strive in making curriculum sense. We agree. However, in describing the next level of effort in curriculum organization, the authors realize that the usual problems of severely limited teacher planning time and meeting time, and problems concerning human relations will loom larger and larger as it becomes necessary to enlarge curriculum scope. With these substantial problems in mind, consider curriculum fitting projects having a scope broader than the single classroom. This is the subject of Chapter 6.

6

Fitting Broad Scope Curriculum

The dust-covered all-school curriculum guide described in Chapter 3 is usually built from the top (all school district), down (through the school level to the individual classroom). This top-down procedure has not worked in the past, and there is no reason to expect it to work in the future. The curriculum building plans in this chapter provide a different process which begins with the simple within-class procedure described in Chapter 5. In this chapter, the within-class curriculum building procedure is gradually expanded to include a between-classes procedure, a between-grade level or within-department procedure, and a within-school procedure. The final curriculum building procedure provided in the chapter is the between schools, or all school district level curriculum building task.

The authors recognize that the curriculum building procedure described in this chapter will be criticized as contrary to at least one ideal curriculum management philosophy which insists that broad school district goals dictate curriculum direction. We present the plan below as a practical procedure through which broad school district goals will evolve through the involvement of teachers and administrators in making a practical educational plan. The procedure is in keeping with human relations principles which counsel that those teachers and administrators affected by action guiding plans should participate in forming the plans. The procedure is in keeping with school management principles which counsel that teacher knowledge of, and acceptance of curricular

77

guidance is maximized when teachers enjoy participation in curriculum formulation.

Fitting Curriculum Between Classes

This section will present a procedure for curriculum fitting among grade levels of an elementary school organization, or among separate class levels within one high school department. By "curriculum fitting" we mean coordination of teaching effort between two or more teachers. Teachers in schools housing two or more sections of the same elementary grade level, or two or more identical secondary school sections (ninth-grade civics) may desire an integration of effort, a constant curricular direction for their entire grade level or subject area. There are eight steps you can take to chart and maintain a common curricular direction.

The first step is to sell the project to professional colleagues. Are the other teachers of your grade level or subject specialty ready to sacrifice some of their autonomy to a collective effort? Can they be brought to a cooperative curriculum project by the potential advantages of shared materials, shared ideas, deliberate direction, collective security, and divided workload? Sell these advantages in your staff lounge chats, and faculty meeting discussions. Status leaders such as department chairmen or principals may wish to initiate such a project as a step toward all-school curriculum planning, or as a desirable end in itself. Whoever initiates the project must remember that any cooperative human effort must be *sold.* The professional jargon speaks primly of "exercising leadership," "providing professional direction," "energizing," "motivating," "involving others," and "inspiring." Face it. Those terms all mean *selling,* and selling is the task of any educator who undertakes to organize his colleagues to a cooperative curriculum building effort.

What are you selling? You are selling the benefits of a common grade or subject curriculum. With a common curriculum you and your colleagues can share materials and ideas among yourselves, and you and your colleagues have the security of numbers in defending your curriculum decisions; you and your colleagues gain the satisfaction of working from professional consensus, rather than personal fiat; and you and your colleagues can divide the workload of lesson planning and materials gathering. These are substantial advantages.

Your buyers get nothing for nothing. Your colleagues must buy these advantages with the hard coin of willingness to participate in grade or subject meetings, reduction of teacher autonomy in curriculum decisions, and acceptance of the principle of compromise to facilitate group decisions. The principle of compromise is particularly difficult for many teachers to accept, for they are dedicated to their work. Nevertheless, for cooperative planning to work, compromise is essential.

Step two requires a meeting. The two or more teachers who are interested in cooperative grade or subject curriculum cooperation need to talk. They may need to formulate a way to involve the school principal or department head in their plan, and they need to talk about the next step.

Step three requires work. It requires following part of the procedure outlined in Chapter 5. Each elementary teacher in the elementary grade level group needs to construct a sample curriculum for one subject (the same subject for each teacher) according to the steps outlined in chapter 5. Each secondary teacher in the "same subject" group needs to construct a sample curriculum for one unit (the same unit for each teacher). This is best done individually by each teacher in preparation for step four.

Step four is another meeting. At this second meeting each teacher will produce his idea of the subject or unit curriculum. With two or more of these proposals on the table for group examination, specific objectives can be criticized or accepted on the basis of the professional judgment of the group members. If all members have done their homework as required, negative criticism and "nit picking" will be absent from this discussion. The discussion will center upon a set of contrary or conflicting specific objectives to be accepted or rejected by the group on the basis of available materials, known achievement levels of learners, pedagogical skill of the teachers, and the values of the community and the teachers. Avoid discussions of what can be done if additional money can be obtained for wonderful, but presently unavailable materials. Focus upon what can be done tomorrow morning with what is immediately available.

Compromise is essential. It is unlikely that you and your

professional colleagues will present identical objectives to the meeting even though your objectives sources are similar or identical. Compromise. Give something, get something.

The meeting (or meetings) should result in a set of specific objectives for the previously selected secondary unit, or elementary grade subject, which are agreeable to all. In homogeneous or tracked organizations for instruction, the levels of proficiency prescribed for pupils should differ according to the achievement levels of the pupils. In heterogeneous organizations, there should be a recognition that some objectives are for all pupils, some will be achieved by only most of the pupils involved.

Once objectives agreement is reached by the group, the business of developing pace estimates is next. This is really a way of assigning importance priorities to various program segments. The teacher who agreed that the objective, "Pupils will be able to write a complete, simple declarative sentence," is important, and who also wishes to meet the objective in two lessons is trying to tell the group something. Be practical. Either allow sufficient time for the objective to be reached by most pupils, or drop the objective from your curriculum. Remember, this curriculum writing business is not an exercise designed to produce a beautiful document to be displayed as a dusty knick-knack; it is designed to produce a practical, useful map for teachers to follow. The only relevant question for the pacing of curriculum is "Can the objectives reasonably be met within our estimate?"

Once the curriculum segment has been paced, you are ready to test it. Try following the curriculum for four or six weeks. Have group members record answers to four questions as they work at the practical task of using the curriculum to guide their teaching efforts:

1. Are materials available to help meet each objective?
2. Do most pupils appear capable of benefiting from the materials and exercises designed to bring them to each objective criterion?
3. Does the pupil performance of the "application" level objectives remain stable outside of the specific testing situations?
4. Is the time allotted for the meeting of each set of objectives realistic?

The next step, step seven, is an evaluation meeting. All members should present their answers to the four questions. These answers will indicate the practicality of the curriculum, and will suggest specific changes needed. Revision of the curriculum in light of teacher experience will serve to make it a practical, useful document.

The seven steps form a beginning to between classes curriculum development. The eighth step is to repeat the whole process for each separate subject or unit considered. The number of meetings required to produce a practical plan serving all teachers involved will vary in inverse proportion to the willingness of the teachers to compromise, and the similarity of teacher viewpoints.

Teacher groups with high compromise potential, and/or similar points of view will find they can write a useful curriculum for a whole year of one secondary subject, or for a year's worth of as many as two elementary school subjects. Attempts at broader accomplishment require either a paid summer workshop for *all* teachers who will use the curriculum, release time for at least one hour per meeting whenever meetings are required, teachers willing to transfer two hours per week of instructional preparation to two hours of cooperative curriculum work, or some combination of the above. In other words, either plan to move very slowly, or plan to rearrange the way you spend your professional time.

Like the single classroom or single subject curriculum, once the between-classes curriculum is completed it is, in itself, ready for immediate use by the teachers who created it. With such a curriculum, each teacher has a coordinated, paced plan to guide instruction. This is an important aid to effective instruction; however, even greater benefit can be derived from the eight steps suggested above.

Discuss your activities with other teachers using the curriculum. What instructional techniques seem to work best in meeting the objectives agreed upon? Explore how one teacher can bring more pupils to meet the objectives than can another. Discover how one teacher can use instructional short-cuts to meet objectives more quickly than can other teachers. Trade ideas on how pupils can be motivated to work toward objectives voluntarily and with relish. Once a common curriculum is a reality, these instructional considerations can be discussed in a practical, immediately useful manner.

Trade materials with other teachers. Since each teacher in the group is working toward the same objectives, teacher-made, teacher-purchased, and teacher-swiped materials are potentially useful to all. This is not intended to limit all teachers to the same materials. It should be recognized that there are different ways to meet identical instructional goals. It should also be recognized that when identical goals are accepted, certain instructional materials become useful to all.

There are eight steps to curriculum fitting between classes. These are:

1. Sell the idea to colleagues.
2. Meet to decide on a test curriculum consisting of a single elementary school subject, or secondary subject unit.
3. Assign each teacher the task of building a list of specific working objectives for the test curriculum.
4. Meet to compare proposed teacher objectives for identical curriculum segments.
5. Compromise. Accept objectives agreeable to all of the teachers involved. Pace the program.
6. Follow the test curriculum for a month or more. Evaluate it according to the four questions.
7. Meet to revise the objectives and the pacing of objectives to comform to what has been discovered in practice.
8. Repeat the previous seven steps as often as needed until a complete between-classes curriculum is available.

Before moving to enlarge the scope of curriculum fitting, it is necessary to treat the matter of teacher replacement once the between-classes curriculum has been organized. Ideally, the between-classes curriculum project is at least coordinated by a principal or department head.[1] However, in case the project is an independent between-class effort on the part of teachers, the administrator who hires teacher replacements must be persuaded to make acceptance of the curriculum a condition of new teacher employment.

As the scope of curriculum is enlarged, the problems in building the curriculum increase. Movement from within class to between classes curriculum was shown to require additional efforts of

---

[1]Dorothy Christine insists this be identified as an administrative prejudice of her co-author.

planning and meeting, and additional skills of selling and compromise. To enlarge curriculum scope beyond the between-classes boundaries to encompass different grade levels in elementary schools, or different subject specialties in high school or lower school departments requires all of the skills and efforts described above, plus more.

Fitting Curriculum at the School or Department Level

The procedure for building an all-school, or all-department level curriculum is essentially the same as the between-classes procedure. The differences between the procedures are differences in size, rather than substance.

The all-school or all-department (department in the sense of either the traditional high school administrative structure, or the elementary school group of grades or team) requires a sophisticated task organization. This task organization will be described in three major steps: (1) preparation for action; (2) curriculum building action; and (3) implementation.

Preparation for Action

This first category of task organization for curriculum building requires coordination among key professionals in the department or elementary school. These professionals must have status, influence with other teachers, and an understanding of the procedures for within-class and between-classes curriculum development as described above. The key professionals should include at least one representative of each subject or grade level that the curriculum will include. The department head and school principal must also be involved in the preparation for action. There are two reasons for inclusion of these professionals. First, the administrators have resources of in-school planning time, secretaries, discretionary budgets, and communications with the whole community which teachers do not have. These resources are needed for large scope curriculum planning. Second, the administrators have the time and the responsibility to supervise the work of teachers. Someone must be charged with the responsibility for overseeing that the completed curriculum is utilized in practice, and the principal or department head is the obvious choice for the job.

The "preparation" procedure needs include meetings between high status teachers and administrators to first decide that a broad scope curriculum will benefit the school, that all are committed to the idea, and that all are willing to work toward realizing it. This group must agree that a successful curriculum writing job will:

1. provide the guidance of a "big picture" to facilitate teacher efforts.
2. provide observable objectives toward which all teachers will move.
3. insure a smooth flow of child intellectual and attitudinal development from level to level.
4. provide teachers with a knowledge of prior instructional efforts so they can:
   a. fill-in gaps in children's knowledge
   b. avoid needless repetition of learning activities
   c. maximize needed repetition of learning activities.
5. avoid conflicting goals among teachers.
6. insure effective curricular observance of the principles of primacy, recency, and reinforcement (see Chapter 1).

Agreement among the members of the preparation group that an organized curriculum will result in some or all of these worthy ends is essential, for it will be the job of the preparation group to move in their respective faculty rooms, boiler rooms, lunch rooms, and meeting rooms to sell an idea. The members of the preparation group will need to sell all teachers who will work within the scope of the proposed curriculum on the idea of working to help make the curriculum.

Prior to embarking on the sales effort, the preparation group, like any successful salesman, must be ready to immediately deliver the product in case it is sold. The product is a plan of action for initiating curriculum development. The three-step plan of action: (1) preparation; (2) curriculum building; (3) and implementation can be graphically prepared in flow chart fashion as shown in Figure 6-1. A more elaborate graphic description of the total effort is provided at the end of this section.

The preparation group also needs to take inventory of the resources which will be available to aid the curriculum building project. Resources which every preparation group should strive to secure are:

1. School psychologist—this functionary, if recently trained, will be able to aid teachers in writing "working objectives."
2. Secretaries—someone needs to transcribe the meeting reports, proposals, memoranda, and drafts which will result from meetings prescribed below.
3. Substitute teachers—someone will need to cover classes for teachers when teachers attend meetings during school hours.
4. Dictating machines—laborious and project killing hours of note taking and proposal writing can be eliminated if a couple of dictaphones (or tape recorders modified with secretarial paks) are secured.
5. Meeting rooms—some meetings will take place while school is in session, and meeting rooms will need to be scheduled.
6. Writing materials—yellow lined legal pads and sharp pencils. Whenever two or more people gather for a meeting, someone forgets a pencil.

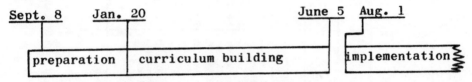

Figure 6-1. Three-Step Plan of Action.

The preparation group for a one-discipline department should plan to spend a minimum of one school year writing a curriculum to cover the entire department. It would not be unrealistic to plan a time span of two years for the project. The preparation group for a cluster of different elementary school grades, or for a total elementary school, will need to decide upon a between-grades curriculum project for no more than a single subject (such as reading), or a group of fused subjects (such as social studies). An attempt at revising the entire elementary or middle school curriculum in a single year is a fast way to create an "exhausted teacher school."

The process described is illustrated in flow chart fashion in Figures 6-2 and 6-3. Figure 6-2 illustrates an hypothetical high school social studies department, Figure 6-3 illustrates a plan for an hypothetical elementary school with a team teaching instructional organization.

	Sept. 8	Sept. 10	Sept. 24	Oct. 9	Oct. 23	Dec. 20	Jan. 20
Mr. Plum, Principal			Consults with Mr. Peach on progress		Aids in selling tough holdouts	Gets necessary school board O. K.	All-department meeting. Formal presentation of plan and formal acceptance or rejection of plan by all dept. teachers.
Mr. Peach, Department Chairman			Calls meetings noted below		Aids in selling tough holdouts		
Mr. Gibbon, History (seniors & juniors)				Reports meeting events to history teachers Attends meetings below	Sells plan to other history teachers		
Mr. Miles, Geography				Reports events to other geography teachers Attends meetings below	Sells plan to other geography teachers		
Mr. Dollar, Economics				Reports events to other department teachers Attends meetings below	Sells plan to remaining dept. teachers		
Participation by whole preparation group listed above.	Explanation of idea of written curriculum to preparation group.	Preparation group members read Chapters One thru Six of this book.	Discussion of plan. Acceptance or rejection of curriculum building plan.	Modification of plan to suit individual situation	Inventory of resources. Clearance by Board of necessary purchases and substitute teachers.		

Figure 6-2. Hypothetical High School Department.

	Sept. 10 – Sept. 12	Sept. 12 – Sept. 26	Sept. 26 – Oct. 11	Oct. 11 – Oct. 25	Oct. 25 – Dec. 20	Dec. 20 – Jan. 20
Mr. Black, Principal		Initiates proposal. Directs meetings.		Gets necessary approval. Aids selling.		Faculty meeting. Formal presentation of plan and acceptance or rejection of plan by all teachers.
Mr. Green, Team Six			Reports meeting events to Team 6 teachers.	Sells Team Six on written curriculum.		
Mrs. White, Team Five			Reports meeting events to Team 5 teachers.	Sells Team 5 on written curriculum.		
Miss Blue, Team Four			Reports meeting events to Team 4 teachers.	Sells Team 4 on written curriculum.		
Mrs. Red, Team Three			Reports meeting events to Team 3 teachers.	Sells Team 3 on written curriculum.		
Mrs. Mauve, Team Two			Reports meeting events to Team 2 teachers.	Sells Team 2 on written curriculum.		
Participation by whole preparation group listed above.	Explanation of idea of written curriculum to preparation group.	Preparation group members read Chapters One thru Six of this book.	Discussion of plan. Acceptance or rejection of curriculum building plan.	Modification of plan to suit individual situation.	Inventory of resources. Clearance by Board of necessary purchases and substitute authorization	

Figure 6-3. Hypothetical Elementary School.

The flow charts end with the formal meeting of all department or teaching team members. Assuming that the project is accepted, the project then moves into the second task organization category—curriculum building action.

Curriculum Building Action

For both the single discipline department (high school, middle school, or upper elementary grades), and the elementary school group of grades the curriculum building action is the same, with one exception. The curriculum workers in the department organization should be able to write a curriculum the scope of which extends over all department classrooms. The curriculum workers in the multi-discipline group of grades will need to limit their scope to a single discipline, or sensible group of fused disciplines. This limitation is suggested so that the job of curriculum building can be completed in a single year without overtaxing the energies of the teacher-curriculum builders.

The curriculum building action process is begun in the manner suggested for the between-classes procedure given at the beginning of the chapter. This will tend to keep work groups small and manageable, as well as provide curriculum objectives proposals which are all couched in about the same style ("working objectives") when the proposals are brought together at later meetings. The leisurely testing of the within-class plans has been eliminated to compress the process to a single half-year.

Since a longer series of meetings is required for the department or school curriculum building effort than was required for the between-classes effort, it is wise to allot one release day for planning to each participant. This release day should be provided in two halves. The first half-day is used for initial planning and organization; the second half-day for final comparison and revision of between-class objectives. It is logical, but not necessary, that the preparation committee members serve as leaders of the between-classes groups, and that they be held responsible for meeting deadlines.

Recall that for between-classes curriculum preparation, the suggestion was made that objectives be built around existing programs and materials. This suggestion is repeated. Many past curriculum building committees have failed precisely because they attempted the Herculean task of building new programs out of whole cloth. Subject, team, or grade level chairmen will need to constantly guard against discussions which drift toward new program writing, and grandiose schemes for rebuilding society.

Once the between-classes curriculums have been completed, it is necessary to duplicate them and distribute copies to all teachers involved in the project. It is necessary for the individuals to study these plans, paying particular attention to the following points:

1. sequential development of skills and attitudes
2. provision of background in basic areas to support more advanced learnings
3. conflicting goals
4. possibilities for synergy.
5. excessive repetition
6. insufficient repetition
7. omissions of essential learnings
8. use of dissimilar symbol systems or terms between subject matter levels without conscious comparison and exposition for pupils.

Several weeks must be allowed for teachers to study the merged between-classes curriculum proposals. Each professional should dictate a formal critique of the proposals, paying particular attention to the subject areas or grade levels closest to his own. These dictated proposals, transcribed by secretaries, form the agendas for additional between-class group meetings. At these meetings, group members need to engage in further discussion and compromise to develop whole-group proposals for specific revisions to make the all-department or all-school plan fit together. Group chairmen will then dictate the agreed-upon revised plans for submission to all other groups. These plans will be studied prior to a meeting of group chairmen, and will form the agenda for a meeting of the group chairmen.

The meeting of group chairmen will consist of discussions of the various revisions, and of compromises to resolve differences. The meeting (or meetings) will result in a department or school curriculum plan acceptable to all of the group chairmen. This plan will be dictated and transcribed, then duplicated, and distributed to all involved professionals. Group chairmen will hold additional meetings with their between-classes groups to either obtain agreement from all teachers that the proposed curriculum is acceptable, or establish areas of irresolvable disagreement. In the event of irresolvable disagreement, the group chairmen will need to reconvene in an attempt to resolve the disagreement. The flow chart in Figure 6-4 describes the curriculum building action program.

Curriculum Implementation

The professionals who will use the department-wide or school-wide curriculum are the same people who built the curriculum. These professionals, by virtue of their involvement in curriculum making, will be familiar with the curriculum and agree with it. Moreover, they will be motivated to use it. Curriculum implementation will be automatic by teachers who participated in creating it.

One problem in curriculum implementation will center upon replacements for teachers who participated in curriculum building, but who resigned their positions following curriculum completion. Initial acceptance of the published curriculum will need to be made a condition of employment for new teachers; furthermore, new teachers will need briefing sessions to insure that they are capable of using the new curriculum as a planning guide.

Briefing sessions, conducted by senior teachers or administrators, should be held prior to school opening. It is essential to the success of the curriculum that these sessions be held either prior to school opening, or during the first two weeks of school. New teachers who are initially allowed to "drift" without direction will tend to resist direction if it is offered later in the year.

Six or eight weeks after school has opened, one or two all-department or all-school meetings need to be held to allow for change in proposals concerning the curriculum. These meetings should be guided by the four questions suggested to guide evaluation of the between-classes curriculum. These questions concerned materials availability, pupil ability, stability of pupils' applications learning, and curriculum pacing. Minor adjustments such as securing materials or pacing alterations can be the immediate result of such a meeting; however, if practice has indicated that major adjustment to the curriculum are needed, then part, or all, of the whole curriculum building process must be repeated.

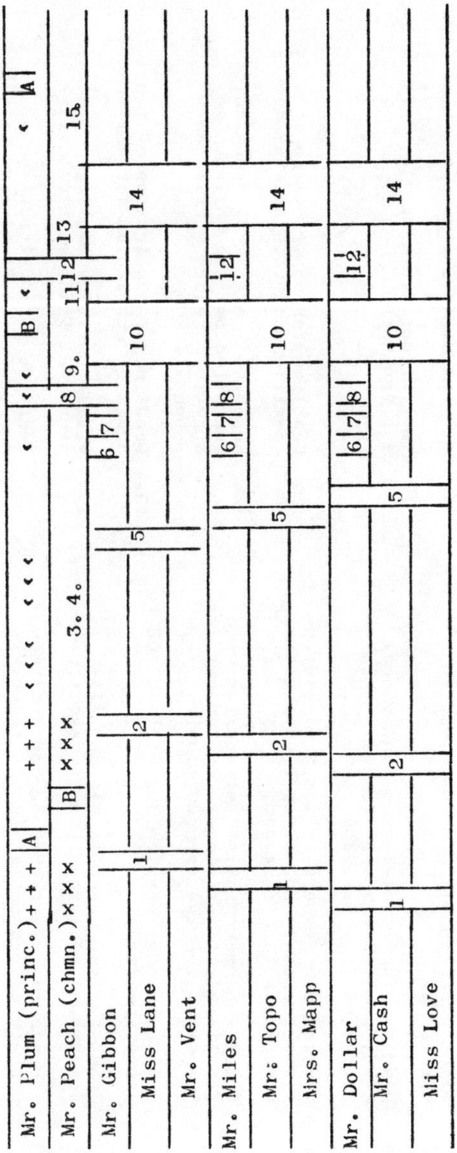

Mr. Plum (princ.) + + + |A| + + +   ✓ ✓ ✓   ✓ ✓ ✓   ✓   ✓ ✓ ✓   ✓ |A|

Mr. Peach (chmn.) x x x |B| x x x   3. 4. |B| ✓   8 9. |B| ✓   11 12   13   15.

Mr. Gibbon   1   2   5   6 7   10   14

Miss Lane

Mr. Vent

Mr. Miles   1   2   5   6 7 8   10   12   14

Mr. Topo

Mrs. Mapp

Mr. Dollar   1   2   5   6 7 8   10   1 12   14

Mr. Cash

Miss Love

Figure 6-4. Flow Chart for Curriculum Building Action Program.

Key to Numerals

1. Initial meeting to describe within-class curriculum objectives proposals.

2. Meeting for members to compare within-class curriculum objectives, and to reach compromise on single between-class plans.

3. Deadline for distribution of all between-class plans to all persons named on chart.

4. Deadline for completion of individual study of between-class plans. Begin dictation of individual comments.

5. Meeting for members to compare between-class proposals and agree upon a plan acceptable to each group.

6. Group Chairmen provide secretaries with finalized all-department curriculums for transcription and reproduction.

7. All-Department curriculums distributed to Group Chairmen.

8. Group Chairmen meet to discuss All-Department revisions and to make compromises.

9. Secretaries distribute "group chairmen curriculum proposals" to all teachers.

10. Reserve time for individual subject group meetings, individual study, and decision for additional curriculum study and revision.

Key to Symbols

+ provide half-day substitute teachers

x provide meeting rooms

< make secretary available for typing and reproduction

A press release describing progress for news media

B description of project for service club luncheon

11. Deadline for distribution of all committee comments to chairmen.

12. Reserve time. Final opportunity for all committee chairmen to accept or reject curriculum proposal.

13. Deadline of duplication of final draft of curriculum for all teachers.

14. Final committee meetings to accept or reject final curriculum.

15. Deadline for distribution of curriculum in final form to all teachers.

Figure 6-4 (continued).

Review School or Department Level Curriculum Fitting

The three processes of preparation, curriculum building, and implementation were described as consuming a time period of fourteen months beginning with preparation committee exploration and ending with all-faculty evaluation. This lengthy project was pointed to constructing a curriculum for either a single department, or a single subject in an elementary school building. The fourteen month time allotment should be considered an absolute minimum, and stretching the time over twenty-four months will be more realistic for many schools.

The time period could be more fully utilized by starting two or more departments or grade level groups simultaneously in the preparation phase. This "doubling up" would not be possible in a teamed or self-contained elementary school organization since the plan is too time consuming for teachers to be able to add to their own teaching and planning the considerable burden of curriculum planning over three or four different subject areas. A complete curriculum plan for the elementary school will require a repetition of the described procedure over a minimum of five one-year cycles. It is highly probable that by the end of the fifth-year cycle the first curriculum constructed will be in need of considerable revision. This is why curriculum writers maintain that elementary school curriculum planning is a continuous process.

Fitting Curriculum on the School Level

Thus far a "from the classroom level to the all-school level" curriculum building scheme has been described. The basic unit of planning, the "white sauce" of the process, has been the within-class, single teacher preparation of a specific objectives listing derived from a commercial program or combination of programs already in use. Where possible, compromises were prescribed to bring each teacher at a common grade level or subject matter class to agree on a common curriculum for heterogeneous pupils organizations or a sensible tracked curriculum for homogeneous pupil organization. The resulting between-classes curriculum was used as a base for building a curriculum of broader scope to encompass each high school department or each subject offered in an entire elementary school.

Once built, the all-school curriculum forms a natural base for all-school curriculum fitting. Such a curriculum, described in terms of "working objectives," is a detailed description of the entire school program. The document can be examined on face to determine whether or not teachers are:

1. reinforcing each other
2. working against one another
3. engaging in excessive repetition
4. providing sufficient repetition
5. assuming a basic skills *application level* of ability which pupils do not have
6. teaching conflicting symbol systems, attitudes, or scientific theories without alerting pupils to the conflicts
7. working to build a level of learning inappropriate to the needs of the pupils (example: building an *application level* of Latin learning, when a *knowledge level* is sufficient)
8. working with concepts sufficiently similar to enable the planning of synergetic learning sequences.

The curriculum fitting procedure can be carried out in the same manner as the curriculum building process described above. The preparation-curriculum building-implementation task organization would only need relabeling to: (1) preparation, (2) curriculum fitting, and (3) implementation. The process described in the Figure 6-4 flow chart is easily adaptable to curriculum fitting. The meeting schedule would need to be changed to accommodate all-department head meetings, for between-departments curriculum decisions, with opportunities to present change proposals to all staff members for ratification prior to final decisions. This change would necessitate shortening the preparation phase to allow an additional two months for the curriculum fitting phase. This may require preparation activities in the summer to insure adequate preparation in difficult situations. The curriculum fitting task-organization is summarized in Figure 6-5.

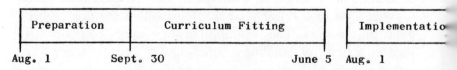

Figure 6-5. Curriculum Fitting Task-Organization.

Fitting Curriculum Between Schools

The curriculum, the document resulting from all of the activities described above, provides officals holding all-school district responsibilities with a living, comparable description of what is going on in the schools. With such a document available, the school board, the superintendent, the curriculum director, and the teachers' association or teachers' union representatives charged with monitoring curriculum can gain a bird's eye view of the direction in which the schools are moving. These officials need to examine the between-schools situation for proper fit in terms of the same eight questions proposed to guide within-school curriculum fitting. Should major changes be deemed necessary to insure proper between-schools curriculum fitting, the high officials have the power to make available the summer or release time for planning needed to insure a district-wide or city-wide fit. Moreover, the high officials have the resources to provide major funding for program changes when it is discovered that certain existing programs cannot be made to fit together.

Should additional curriculum change be necessary to insure a proper between-school fit, a system such as the previously described curriculum building task organization would be required to make the change. This would assure both teacher understanding of the changes, and teacher consent for the changes.

In the event that a program change is needed to either replace an outdated program, or to improve between-schools curriculum fit, the "working objectives" curriculum would provide a concrete, practical basis for making a decision from among available programs. This would change the decision basis of the program selection group from the too frequent question of "which salesman has the nicest smile?" to the more professional question of "which program fits best into our curriculum?"

Summary

Chapters 5 and 6 have described curriculum building. These two chapters have proposed concrete, practical measures which can be put into practice immediately at any level of school organization. The classroom teacher can construct his own plan with a minimum expenditure of time, and no expenditure of money. A group of teachers sharing similar educational responsibilities can cooperate to produce a curriculum of slightly broader scope, but with little more expenditure of time than the teacher working in isolation.

Greater investments of time and cooperation with fellow professionals will produce curriculums to cover whole departments, or whole elementary and middle schools. At this level, the benefits of proper between-grades curriculum fit result from the extra effort.

On the base of the larger scale curriculum building efforts, multi-department schools, and school districts can move to achieve the educational ideal of an integrated, all-school district curriculum which is both utilizable and utilized by teachers.

7

Keep Your Curriculum
Materials Current

The curriculum building schemes suggested previously operate from the base of curriculum materials already in existence in your school. These curriculum building schemes were presented as a practical solution to an often encountered problem met by professionals who are ready to build curriculum at a time when their boards of education are not ready to spend money to buy new programs. A related problem is the happy situation when boards of education are ready to spend money for curriculum materials. This chapter outlines programs which will help you to spend the money wisely.

The happy money spending times usually appear when professionals are least ready for them. Money, particularly federal money, is too often offered to teachers on a "crash" basis, to be spent for a specific purpose within a few months after it is made available. Special state grants in aid, foundation contributions, or even suddenly discovered pockets of local money descend upon principals and teachers with an urgency to spend only slightly less pressing than the federal windfalls. Preparations for wisely spending this money to fit your curriculum must be made now. Now, as you sit quietly reading, some board member or legislator may be acting to shower you with cash to be spent before the end of the calendar year, fiscal year, or next new moon. Are you ready to spend the money wisely?

Suggestions for Curriculum Sources Management

If any of the curriculum building and/or curriculum fitting programs described in previous chapters have been initiated or completed for your area of responsibility, then you are "half ready" to make wise decisions for curriculum materials purchases. You are "half ready" in that you know what is needed to enhance, expand, or change the direction of your curriculum. Half of the job of wise selection is knowing what is needed; the other half is knowing what is available.

Hundreds of manufacturers and suppliers of curriculum materials worry about getting information to you concerning their wares. Materials makers debate constantly the best means for telling their stories to professionals who use the materials. Salesmen for these companies court you at conventions, flood your mail with catalogs and pamphlets, call on you at school, pepper your professional journals with promotional materials, and bury your boss with samples.

So much information is available describing so many programs offered by literally hundreds of suppliers that busy professionals suffer "cognitive strain" trying to assimilate this information. Avoid "brain strain." Don't assimilate the descriptive materials; organize them. Organize descriptions of what materials are available so that the next time your principal or superintendent announces the appearance of a great windfall of spendable cash you can calmly hand him an order describing exactly what you need, what it costs, and who makes it.

The remainder of this chapter contains descriptions of practical methods of curriculum information organization: the file, the cross-index, the key index, and automatic data processing.

Avoid the Pile

Most schools already have this system. It is not recommended. "The Pile" is the disorganized stack of catalogs, pamphlets, and clippings in the teacher's or principal's closet. Usually the keeper of the pile has a rough idea of what it contains, and, given several hours of pawing through dust covered catalogs, can even find a few sources of desired curriculum materials. The pile can be maintained by anyone from the school secretary to the curriculum director. The school secretary can be excused for maintaining the pile—she doesn't need curriculum materials information. You do.

How to Use the File

The file is an alphabetical organization of supplier's catalogs and pamphlets in a file cabinet. All promotional materials from each supplier are filed under the supplier's name, from Adirondack to Zayer. Avoid trying to simply stack catalogs and pamphlets in the file naked. Give each supplier the courtesy of a manila file folder inscribed with his name. The file folder will insure that fat catalogs and thin pamphlets from the same supplier will tend to stay together.

Weed. Many suppliers send duplicates of their catalogs and pamphlets in different mails. Duplicate materials are rarely needed in a principal's or department head's file, and never needed in a teacher's file. Moreover, catalogs from even sleepy suppliers are issued yearly; therefore, whenever you add material to a file folder, remove outdated material.

The file is a basic information retrieval system which organizes information for you, but does nothing to help you find the information at a later date. If, as a teacher, you wish to find a level three reading program to supplement your primary program you may recall that file folders marked "Scott-Foresman" or "Ginn" contain helpful suggestions. You may also forget that file folders marked "Stanwix" or "Educational Developmental Laboratories" also contain suggestions. To consider all possibilities you will need a better system than the file.

How to Use the Cross-Index

To recall the less obvious possibilities you need an "automatic memory." One such device is the cross-index.

The cross-index need be no more than a pack of three by five inch file cards. The name of each materials supplier is written on each card, and a short notation of the grade level applicability and subject matter relevancy of the supplier's wares is written below the supplier's name. Figure 7-1 shows a sample cross-index card.

A cross-index for a single subject teacher may contain only a few dozen cards. A cross-index maintained by a department head or a school principal will contain several hundred cards.

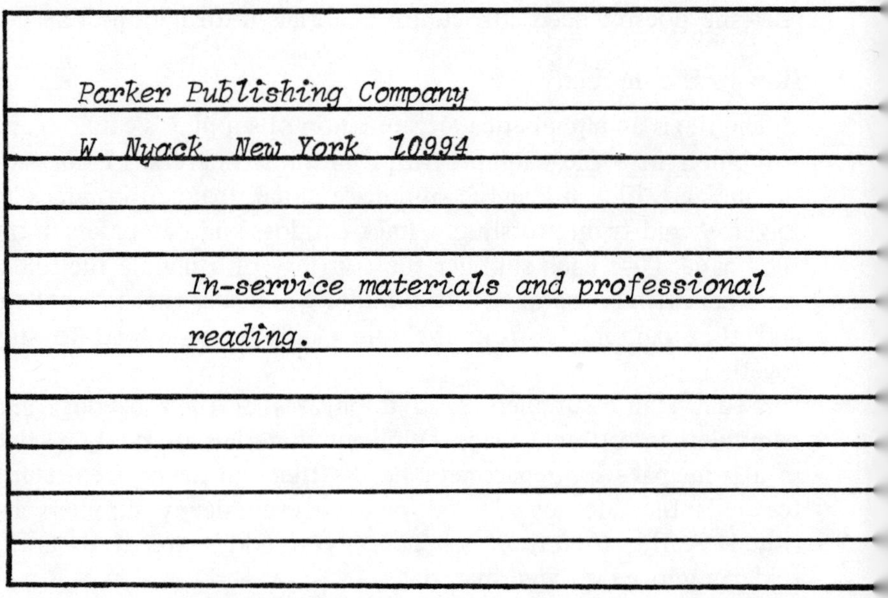

```
Parker Publishing Company
W. Nyack  New York  10994



      In-service materials and professional
      reading.
```

Figure 7-1. Sample Cross-Index Card.

Since cross-index maintenance does require expenditures of time, it is wise to keep a single cross-index for an entire school building. It should be noted that if the school principal is unwilling to maintain such a system, individual teachers can set up small personal indexes. However, much efficiency is gained if one cross-index is kept by the principal for all teachers and team or department leaders.

The cross-index cannot be wholly maintained by the principal's secretary. School secretaries simply do not have the background in curriculum necessary to the upkeep of a satisfactory index. There is much the secretary can do to aid in building, maintaining, and using the cross-index, but professional attention to the task is essential.

The first step in building a cross-index is to establish a file of materials suppliers (see "The File"). Following establishment of the file, the school secretary should type the name and address of each supplier represented in the file on a three by five index card. The third step necessitates having a professional educator scan the contents of each supplier's file, and summarize the contents on the supplier's index card. Summaries should be organized according to subject matter and achievement level designations for the materials offered by the supplier. Special interests (such as team teaching) of individual faculties may dictate additional notations over and above subject and achievement levels; however, subject matter and achievement level designations are basic to the cross-index system.

Supporting materials such as school furniture, office supplies, individual teacher supplies, and even cleaning supplies can be included in the same cross-index file system as is used for curriculum materials. With such a system it matters little how large the basic file grows since there will be no need for "pawing through the pile" once the index cards have been completed.

The complete cross-index pack of three by five cards can be used by the school secretary or teacher aide as a source of information to search whenever a professional educator requests specific curriculum materials data. For example, if it becomes necessary for a committee of teachers to research level six arithmetic materials in preparation for the purchase of such materials, the school secretary can be instructed to scan the cross-index cards, remove all cards marked both "arithmetic" and "level six," find the matching suppliers' folders in the catalogs file, and deliver the appropriate file folders to the committee chairman. Lest this card scanning chore sound formidable, we hasten to add that a slow school secretary learns to scan the index cards at about one card per second. Assuming a pack of three hundred cards, the whole scanning job requires only five minutes of secretary time. This five minutes of secretary time will yield more materials information for professionals than will five hours of teacher time spent pawing through the unorganized piles of catalogs maintained in some schools.

The cross-index needs not only to be built, but it needs to be maintained. Some professional, preferably the school principal or his assistant, must scan the new promotional materials weekly to update the files and index cards. He must also create new file locations and index cards as new publishers announce their birth, and he must relegate junk materials (ads for candy promotions, cheap ditto reproductions, and photograph sales) to the waste-basket. This updating project consumes about fifteen well-spent minutes per week, and much less if only a one-subject teacher file is being maintained.

The cross-index is the least expensive (considering initial set-up costs) usable curriculum materials control system possible. Installation of the system for a school requires three to eight file cabinet drawers, several hundred file folders, several packs of three by five inch index cards, and two days of principal and secretary time. Installation of the system for a single classroom requires only the teacher will to set it up, and an hour or two of teacher time.

The success of the cross-index pivots on the ability of the school secretary or teacher aide to carefully scan a large number of three by five cards in a short amount of time. Error is always possible when such a rote task is undertaken, and there are mechanical ways to insure greater accuracy. For those who wish greater accuracy, and greater speed in curriculum materials information access, the key index may be the answer.

How to Use the Key Index

Use of the key index is not recommended for individual teachers. This type of system is designed to handle the great quantities of curriculum materials data found at the building, school district, or school district area service facility level.

The key index system begins, as do all curriculum materials systems described, with the establishment of the file explained earlier in this chapter. Once the file is established, it is necessary to secure a "key card system" from a supplier such as Fred C Behrens or Doubleday.[1]

The key card systems consist of several hundred "key cards" as pictured in Figure 7-2, a little paper punch supplied with the cards, and several "needles" to stick through the holes in the cards.

The first step in establishing the key index is to title one key card for each supplier represented in the file in the same manner as was described in setting up the three by five card cross-index. The second step is to summarize the contents of each file folder on the key cards noting subject relevancy and instructional level applicability. The next step will require initial help from whoever supplies your key cards. Key card suppliers not only make set-up assistance available, but almost insist that they be involved in initial system

[1]Fred C. Behrens. 3732 W. Twelfth Street, Erie, Pennsylvania, 16505.

Doubleday Brothers and Company. 1919 E. Kilgore Rd. Kalamazoo, Michigan, 49001.

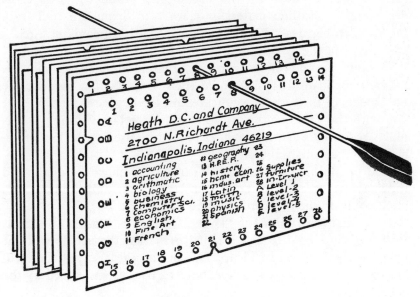

Figure 7-2.

establishment. The key card suppliers do this because they recognize the complexity of the initial set-up task, and they are dependent upon your satisfaction for future sales. Use their help. Ask your key card supplier to scan this chapter, and he will recognize what needs to be done. Discuss your unique curriculum materials information needs with the representative and allow him to suggest additional dimensions for the key index system beyond the basic three dimensional *subject matter by achievement level by publisher name* system suggested in the cross-index section. Even the simplest key index system can handle more than three dimensions with ease, and you may wish to gain the benefits of more specific indexing such as price limitations, within subject program limitations, or across-level subject continuity limitations.

Once established, the key index system will do away with the need for your secretary to scan several hundred cards each time a professional needs curriculum materials information. For example, if you wish to discover the materials and programs available for Spanish II, the school secretary would simply insert a key index needle in the card pack hole marked "Spanish." By suspending the cards above her desk by the needle she would cause all cards describing curriculum materials relevant to Spanish to fall from the pack to her desk. By assembling the Spanish cards in a pack, and inserting the needle in the card pack hole marked "level 2" the secretary could retrieve cards designating suppliers of materials relevant to Spanish II. she would then go to the file, remove the file folders of the suppliers indicated on the key cards, and present you with the file folders that you need. Secretary working time is much reduced over the scanning procedure used with the "cross-index" and accuracy is increased.

You get nothing for nothing. With the key index there is a need for increased secretary time in translating your card summaries to punch-outs on the key cards as shown in Figure 7-3.

Note that the holes for "level 2" and for "Spanish" are cut from the card hole to the card edge so that the needle will not hold the card shown in Figure 7-3, and all cards so punched will fall out of the card pack when the card pack is suspended by the needle alone.

o 1	o 2	o 3	o 4	o 5	o 6	o 7	o 8	o 9	o 10	o 11	o 12	o 13	o 14

o A   _Heath, D. C. and Company_   o

◝ B   _2700 N. Richardt Ave._

o C   _Indianapolis, Indiana 46219_   o

1	accounting	12	geography	23	
2	agriculture	13	H.P.E.R.	24	
3	arithmetic	14	history	25	
4	biology	15	home econ.	26	supplies
5	business	16	indust. art	27	furniture
6	chemistry	17	Latin	28	in-service
7	computer sci.	18	math	A	level 1
8	economics	19	music	B	level 2
9	English	20	physics	C	level 3
10	fine art	21	Spanish	D	level 4
11	French	22		E	level 5

o D   o
o E   o
o F   o
o G   o
o H   o

15	16	17	18	19	20	21	22	23	24	25	26	27	28
o	o	o	o	o	o	⌒	o	o	o	o	o	o	o

Figure 7-3. Spanish II Key Card Example.

It is not necessary to restrict each card to only one achievement level, or one subject. Indeed, some cards for large supply houses may have nearly all of the key card holes punched to the edge, since these are comprehensive suppliers. An elementary school example of such a situation is given in Figure 7-4.

		o			o	o		o				o		o
1	2	3	4	5	6	7	8	9	10	11	12	13	14	

A

Science Research Associates

I

B

259 E. Erie Street

C

Chicago, Illinois 60611

J o

D	1	arithmetic	12	State hist.	23	furniture	
E	2	art	13	spelling	A	KINDERGART.	K o
	3	audio-vis.	14	toys/games	B	LEVEL I	
	4	English	15		C	LEVEL II	
	5		16		D	LEVEL III	L o
F	6	H.P.E.R.	17		E	LEVEL IV	
	7	in-service	18		F	LEVEL V	
	8	penmanship	19		G	LEVEL VI	M o
G	9	reading	20		H	LEVEL VII	
	10	science	21	tchr. sups.	I	LEVEL VIII	
H	11	soc. studs.	22	maint.	J		N o

15	16	17	18	19	20	21	22	23	24	25	26	27	28
	o	o	o	o	o	o	o	o	o	o	o	o	o

Figure 7-4. Elementary School Key Card Example.

Notice that in Figure 7-4 the card for Science Research Associates is represented in any achievement level search, and in searches involving any of the nine subject matter categories.

Guidelines for ADP Curriculum Sources Management

Any task which can be accomplished by cross-index or key index techniques can also be done by automatic data processing equipment. Automatic Data Processing (ADP) machines, like the key index system, can deliver a pack of selected cards representing specific curriculum materials suppliers, or they can print a list of suppliers' names from data stored in a non-card memory such as drum or tape storage. Obviously, not even a multi-school curriculum director can afford to purchase and install ADP equipment solely for the purpose of cataloging curriculum materials information

However, many secondary schools, area vocational schools, and junior colleges are installing ADP equipment for administrative or training purposes. Usually the capacity of ADP equipment of this nature is underused, and "time" on locally available equipment is waiting for school personnel who know how to ask for it. Know how to ask for "time" on locally available ADP equipment.

The IBM 1620 and the IBM 1130 are popular training machines. These ADP models, and similar machines from other companies can be easily programmed to do the card sorting tasks described in this chapter. The program writing phase of a curriculum materials supplier locator system can be accomplished by many high school students as a worthwhile training project in the use of the 1620. In addition, all IBM sales offices have programmers on call to construct such programs for a small fee as a service to customers. We hasten to add that it is a rare school district which does not have at least one parent who is both in the programming business and willing to donate his services for such a project.

Experience has shown that few programmers are willing to settle for the simple three dimensional system (level by subject by supplier) described above, and they are usually right. Even simple ADP machines are capable of more than three clean decisions. You can afford to get a bit more discriminating with the ADP systems than with the cross-index or key index. However, bear in mind, as your programmer speaks of infinite decision possibilities, that ADP machines must get their initial and update information from somewhere. The "somewhere" source of information is you, or a professional assistant, marking little "x's" on ADP cards. The key index information input was estimated at fifteen minutes per week for a three dimensional system, with added time required for additional dimensions. ADP will require the same amount of decision making and card marking time, and the job cannot be done by a nonprofessional. Curriculum directors will undoubtedly wish to add additional dimensions to the basic three, and they should. School principals are wise to severely limit the discriminability of their ADP systems to four or five dimensions.

Review Curriculum Sources Management

A curriculum composed of working objectives and pace estimates for your class, grade, department or school is half of what you need to make wise decisions for the purchase of instructional materials. To complete your bases for purchasing decisions you also need to know what instructional materials are available.

A pile of catalogs in a closet is not much help to aiding your purchasing decisions. A first step in curriculum materials sources management is to organize all available catalogs into an alphabetized physical file.

Catalogs and pamphlets organized in an alphabetized file make teacher and principal access to curriculum materials sources easier than pawing through "the pile." However, materials sources listed in a manual cross-index made of three by five cards insures that forgotten materials sources in the file will not be overlooked, and the cross-index allows for rapid recovery of materials sources descriptions.

For large collections of materials sources information, such as the school principal or district curriculum director needs, the key-index offers advantages of faster and more accurate materials sources access than does the manual cross-index. Similar advantages of speed and accuracy were held for the ADP systems over the key index system.

Whatever system you choose, use it to aid in making curriculum materials decisions in advance of school district cash availability. Do this, and when the cash becomes available you will have a "shopping list" ready to insure that the cash is used rapidly, but professionally.

8

Essentials of Instruction

Introduction to Practical Instructional Considerations

This chapter forms an introduction to the "Instruction" section of this book. Like Chapter 1, certain general principles are developed here for their own practical value, and as a groundwork for specific use in later chapters.

The chapter first identifies "instruction" as a specific activity within the set of activities called "teaching." Next, the chapter presents a bifurcate classification of all instructional acts as either managerial tasks pointed to managerial goals, or substantive tasks pointed to substantive goals. Examples of Carol, who neglected managerial tasks, and of Joan and Keith who refined their managerial task accomplishment provide practical demonstrations of the importance of the managerial-substantive distinction.

A system which will help you gain more time for the achievement of substantive goals is detailed in the chapter. The chapter closes with a practical discussion of the misunderstood concepts of "teaching" and "learning."

Instruction and Teaching

You are a teacher. Regardless of whether your official title is classroom teacher, helping teacher, specialist, curriculum director, principal, or superintendent, you are a teacher. You are a teacher because you are planning activities whose goal is learning on the part of children or adults. You are a teacher because you are also engaged in activating those planned activities. As you activate learning activities, as you personally contact learners in the ancient personality to personality procedure of skills passing, information giving, and attitude building, you are doing the specific act of *instructing.* As we speak of instruction, we speak of the ancient act of skills passing, information giving, and attitude building.

Managerial Goals and Substantive Goals

When your instruction is pointed toward aiding learners in developing a background they will need to gain to qualify for further schooling, to interact with people outside the school setting, to make their lives more satisfying, or to earn a living, then your instruction is pointed to the fulfillment of *substantive goals.* These are the substance of the curriculum. Substantive goals form the reasons for bothering to instruct. The tutor to an individual learner concentrates almost solely upon achieving substantive goals. Few modern professionals are tutors to individual children; therefore, teachers who find that learners are delivered in groups of thirty or forty must work to fulfill *managerial goals* as well as substantive goals.

Managerial goals are achieved when the teacher of many learners finds his learners of a mind to learn by way of the learning activity at hand. The managerial task is to structure the learning situation so that learners know what they are about to learn, have the materials they will need, have some desire to participate in the learning activity, are capable of participating in the learning activity, and have a classroom climate where learning is possible. None of this structuring, materials distribution, motivating, or participation facilitating has a direct relationship to the substance of instruction. Nevertheless, without the structure, materials, motivation, or participation, substantive goals never are reached. Carol learned this from her hectic first day as a teacher.

Carol had carefully prepared for her first day as a third-grade teacher. She had arranged her furniture in cozy groups, avoiding the traditional straight rows that had been labeled by her college teacher as "old fashioned," "traditional," and "authoritarian." Carol's bulletin boards were neat and colorful, evoking both memories of the summer past, and anticipations for the approaching autumn. There were teasing hints to the children of science and social studies materials that would stimulate both interest and involvement in the work. The plans upon Carol's desk were carefully prepared, listing both learning objectives and activities for meeting the objectives. Finally, that hoped for, and feared for, day arrived.

Carol's classroom began to fill with children and parents. Her class looked less ordered, less controlled, than did her class in prior fantasies of quiet, busy groups of intellectually active children. Carol's composure was shaken by the attractive young mother who breezily quipped, "Well, Well. Your vacation has ended, but my vacation is just beginning."

Indeed, the lady's eight year old did have a look of malevolence in his eye—an energetic malevolence. Carol began to wonder if she would survive until lunch. Suddenly she realized that she didn't know the location of the lunchroom.

Further memories of that day are a nightmarish jumble for Carol. There were child stampedes to the pencil sharpener, requests for drinks and more drinks, multiple bathroom visits by all children, and angry calls from the public address system for lunch count lists, attendance reports, milk monies, and children to be delivered to the assembly room to meet the principal. The day was a blur of children in all conceivable sizes, shapes, colors, temperaments, interests, and abilities. Long before dismissal time Carol's well ordered substantive plans were buried beneath a mass of notices, lists, teacher's manuals, and papers. Several times during the day Carol was forced to retreat to her coat closet, appearing to seek some needed paper, but really to compose her shattered nerves. Carol felt that only the dismissal bell saved her from a totally hopeless situation.

Carol didn't know it then, but she later realized that her first teaching day experiences were shared by many beginning teachers, and the experiences did not mean that she was doomed to be a hopeless flop as a teacher. Sure, she had to retreat to the coat closet on several occasions in order to compose herself, but having survived this temporary exile she later emerged as an assured and competent teacher. One thing that Carol learned, under the tutelage of master teachers, was to make a distinction between substantive and managerial goals. This helped Carol out of the coat closet, and into control of sensible classroom managerial tasks.

Some teachers never learn. Consider the classrooms that you have seen where the teacher must constantly call for order, where learners frequently badger the instructor with irrelevant questions, where the handing-in of lesson paper is always surrounded by confusion and disorder. These are classrooms where too little attention has been paid to managerial goals. This lack of managerial attention results in a great amount of valuable time being spent on managerial tasks which should be spent in pursuit of substantive goals.

The instruction of learners in classroom procedures, deportment, and behaviors facilitative to group instruction is not wasted time. It is time well-spent in organizing managerial tasks which will yield time-saving (and teacher saving) dividends in creating a classroom climate conducive to learning.

Test Your Organization Skills

Try this. Ask a colleague (or a bright high school pupil) to sit in on your next instructional performance. Call him your *observer.* Give your observer a watch with a second hand and ask him to keep a record of how much time you spend accomplishing managerial tasks, and how much time you spend working to fulfill substantive goals.

Pick a time of year when you think that your class is well organized, say November or April. Teach your observer the distinction between substantive goals and managerial goals. Let your observer know exactly what you intend to teach so he can easily discriminate between what is substantive and what is managerial for the particular learning activity. Then let your observer record, for the duration of one lesson, the number of minutes you spend working to achieve substantive goals. Most teachers who have done this have been quite surprised at the large amount of time they spend on managerial tasks. Can you find ways to reduce managerial tasks accomplishment time? Joan Weld did.

Using Goals Distinction to Increase
Instructional Efficiency

Joan Weld was part of a third-grade teaching team. She was responsible for the language arts instruction given seventy-five third-grade pupils. An important part of this instruction was the gradual transfer from manuscript to cursive writing. Joan found that the managerial aspects of this writing instruction were consuming between a quarter and a half of her total time spent in writing instruction. Joan felt that paper passing, pencil replacing, instructions repeating, and the creation of blackboard demonstrations were robbing her of time which should be spent giving individual help to children.

When she took a hard look at her instruction (with the aid of an observer), Joan noted that she had repeated identical instructions for lesson completion three times to her three different classes. She had also written nearly identical instructions three times on the blackboard for her classes.

Joan decided to reduce the amount of time spent in instructions repeating and chalkboard writing. For future writing lessons Joan prepared lesson instructions and examples on ditto sheets, and provided room on the sheets for children to do their work. She was able to place tracing exercises, letter formation models, and practice models on these worksheets. After one paper passing, each child had both an instruction sheet and practice sheet. Moreover, Joan was free from the start of the period to begin giving individual help to children. As she continued this program, Joan found that she could use past, preplanned lessons to aid children having difficulty with a particular letter, and the past lesson packages also helped in bringing children who were absent up to date when they returned to school.

Joan Weld gained a little time for working toward substantive goals with some ingenuity and a ditto machine. So did Keith Sloane, but his problem was larger than Joan's.

Keith Sloane is a ninth-grade math teacher in Collins Junior High. At the beginning of his second year of teaching Keith was assigned a "special" math class. Students in the class ranged from those who could barely accomplish subtraction solutions to a few who could actually solve examples in division with two digit divisors. When Keith had his observer stop by, he was attempting to use the "commercial arithmetic" text supplied him by his department head as his sole instructional aid. The observer, somewhat harried by the need to guard her eyes against the assaults of paper airplanes sailing toward her each time Keith turned to write on the chalkboard, managed to record a math period in which Keith spent ten minutes working toward the substantive goal of building arithmetic skills, thirty-five minutes working on managerial goals of trying to keep the pupils orderly and superficially interested in the subject of arithmetic. Keith quickly realized that a ten minute per day math period was too short.

Keith discussed the matter with his department head, and formulated a plan to increase his substantive tasks working time. The first step of the plan involved dropping any attempt at substantive task accomplishment for as long as it took to accomplish the managerial task of gaining the pupil's cooperation in working to improve their arithmetic skills. For Keith's group this involved the holding of nine forty-five minute "bull sessions" many of which Keith was able to steer to the importance of arithmetic in occupational endeavors—legal and illegal. While the bull sessions progressed, Keith worked on developing a series of fifty mimeographed work-sheets presenting either a number of examples or problems. The sheets were graded from simple subtraction, through the other processes of arithmetic, to some simple operations with fractions. Keith laid out the sheets so that the solution lines formed a pattern if the correct solutions were filled in. In this way he could tell at a glance when an example or problem was solved incorrectly. Keith also laid out the sheets so that individual columns of examples on the example sheets contained different opportunities for a pupil to make the same type of mistake. For example, one column of one of the multiplication sheets displayed the following examples:

305	203	304	607	202	605	302
X6	X9	X6	X3	X9	X3	X6

Since the solutions declined by three Keith could correct the solutions at a glance. Keith also knew that if a pupil consistently found incorrect solutions to the examples, then the pupil may be having a problem in dealing with the n-zero-n multiplicand.

Keith carefully laid the *managerial* ground work for having the pupils accept the sheets by (1) selling the pupils on the practicality of the program as preparation for future jobs, (2) assuring the pupils that he would help them to succeed in completing the sheets, (3) assuring the pupils that for the first time in their lives they had an opportunity to get a decent "grade" in math, and (4) telling the pupils that they need not work on the sheets during "off days" so long as they did not disturb others interested in getting ahead. Keith also cautioned the pupils that the work would seem easy at first, but they would get all the challenge they wanted as they progressed through the program. He completed the preparation by insisting upon proper numeral formation in writing answers.

On the day he distributed his first mimeographed sheet, Keith established careful procedures for distributing the exercises, distributing pencils (the pupils never brought them), signaling for his attention to check a paper, and signaling for his attention for help.

Keith found the program worked well. Most of the pupils were able to complete the early subtraction and multiplication sheets without aid, leaving Keith free to help individuals, and small groups where possible, with difficulties. As each pupil worked to the end of his arithmetic knowledge, Keith could spot where that end was since the example columns were carefully laid out for diagnostic purposes.

Keith spent nine forty-five minute periods laying managerial groundwork for his program, and the program solved most, but by no means all of his managerial problems. He still spent fifteen minutes during each period making calls for order, or correcting misbehaving pupils. Nevertheless, Keith's attention to the managerial tasks of the teaching job provided his class with thirty minutes per day devoted to achieving substantive math goals, a net gain of twenty minutes over what he got previously when he had managed his managerial tasks haphazardly.

Working to achieve managerial goals with a minimum of time and effort paid off for Carol and Keith. It can pay off for you, too.

Use the Teaching-Learning Concept

Recall the definition of *teaching* given in Chapter 1. Teaching is the activation of the curriculum plan toward the object of causing a change in pupil behavior.

Recall the Chapter 1 description of *learning*. Four levels of learning were identified to make clear the types of pupil behavior changes you should look for while doing all of the things we call teaching.

Take a look at teaching and learning together, as they are

presented in this section. Teaching and learning are descriptive concepts which converge at the personality to personality meeting of instructor and pupil. Of course, it is possible for a pupil to learn without the intervention of consciously planned teaching by someone, or by some didactic device. Learning can be, and often is the result of something other than planned instruction (teaching). Learning is an object in itself, and not necessarily the result of planned instruction. However, teaching is not an object in itself, and teaching depends for its success upon the attainment of its object—learning.

Failure to recognize this teaching-learning relationship is as devastating an error to a teacher's success as was the failure of the new teacher to discriminate between her bowling lane and ours. Of course, you want to achieve a beauty and finesse in curriculum planning and instructional style that is worthy of producing both outside admiration and inner satisfaction. But the object of our game is to stimulate learning. Without the event of your pupil's learning, your most polished, most elegant performance is as objectless as the student teacher's staged performance for the weekly visit of his supervisor.

Professor Gourevich, of Temple University, once interrupted a complicated lecture, during which student attention was obviously flagging. To reawaken his students Dr. Gourevich boomed in his authorative bass, "I can teach this material to you, but I can't learn it for you!"

The exclamation shocked Dr. Gourevich's students to attention. It also is a statement illustrative of the teaching-learning relationship.

You can teach. Probably you teach effectively, even elegantly. Nevertheless, if the teaching, or if the learning objectives toward which the teaching is pointed are inappropriate to learners, for reasons inherent to learners, then learning will not take place. Then it is time to "back up" and replan.

When you find yourself "trying to learn it for them," do this. First, determine that your teaching is appropriate to the learners' present level of learning. Second, insure that you have successfully met sufficient managerial goals to permit, or induce, your pupils to meet you somewhere between the point where your teaching ends and their learning begins. Finally, examine your substantive goals. Recognize that it is sometimes impossible to pass certain learnings to certain pupils at certain times, that you can't "learn it for them."

Consider the engineers. Engineers in modern America have made the old cliches about moving mountains meaningless. Today, engineers do move mountains, and they achieve lots of other useful goals as well. However, engineers work within a defined technology. Engineers know that they can move mountains, and they accept mountain moving commissions. Engineers know that they cannot build perpetual motion machines, and honest engineers decline perpetual motion machine building commissions. Teachers, who point their efforts to objects far more sensitive than mountains or machines, can afford to do no less.

Any set of descriptions of learning, or prescriptions for instructing such as are in the following chapters of this book should be prefaced by a caution against attempting to force learners to do what they cannot, or will not do. The above paragraph is such a preface.

Review the Essentials of Instruction

Teaching is a generic term encompassing the activities of curriculum planning, materials buying, instructing, and more. *Instructing* is a specific activity through which the teacher passes skills, gives information, and builds attitudes in pupils. Specific techniques for successful instructing are presented in the remaining chapters of this book.

Most teachers expect that instruction will be pointed to the accomplishment of the substantive goals, which are the meat of the curriculum. However, Carol discovered that concentration on substantive goals alone is not sufficient to their accomplishment. It is also necessary to give attention to managerial goals, the things that contribute to classroom order and smooth operation. The use of a classroom observer to record the amount of time he devoted to managerial tasks helped Keith Sloane to improve his instruction. It may help you in a similar manner.

The relationship between teaching and learning is delicate, and difficult to conceptualize. However, as teachers implement the techniques presented in this chapter and subsequent chapters, the teacher-learning concept will aid teachers in making sensible use of the instructional techniques, as well as serving as caution that no teacher, regardless of technique, "can learn it for them."

9

Use an Eclectic Approach to
Learning Process

The Practical Value of an Eclectic Approach

You hear a good deal of talk about *learning theory*. The usual singular form of the term implies that there is *a* learning theory. There is not *a* learning theory. There are notions about how people learn called *learning theories,* and there are many of them.

Learning theories are discussed in this chapter from the standpoint of how they can help teachers to improve instruction. The chapter also counsels professionals to remember that different learners often learn in different ways. The learning theory that seems to offer insights into how best to teach John, may offer no clues to guide the instruction of Mary. John and Mary learn in different ways. Similarly, the practical insights that emanate from one learning theory may provide useful teaching strategies when the object of teaching is mathematics learning, yet provide no help when the object of teaching is poetry appreciation.

When teachers seek practical instructional guidance from the catalogue of learning theories, they must select the theory that makes sense for their pupils, their teaching objectives, and their own personalities.

The necessity for great care when dealing with theory is demonstrated by the story of the fly dissection. The story begins in a laboratory where the students pressed closely about the dissection station occupied by their professor, a leading researcher and theorist. The professor was operating upon a wingless fly he had entrapped on his table. The professorial voice called, "Jump!" and the fly jumped, to the fascinated gaze of the students. Majestically, the professor seized the fly, and removed one of its six legs. Placing the fly back on the table, the professor commanded, "Jump!" and released the fly. Again the fly jumped. The students glanced rapidly from professor to fly. Again the dissector seized the fly and removed another of its legs. Again he commanded the fly to jump, and the fly jumped. The professor repeated the process again and again until he had removed five of the fly's six legs, and each time the fly, indeed, jumped.

Following removal of the fly's sixth leg the professor placed the fly on the table, commanded it to jump, and released the tortured Muscidae who wriggled helplessly on the table. "Observe," said the professor to his students, "as predicted by my auralentric theory and demonstrated here, when one removes all legs from a fly it then loses its sense of *hearing.*"

You do not need a background in research design to surmise that the professor's conclusion was reached through a maximum of prejudice and a minimum of reason. It is easy to objectively evaluate speculations concerning the behavior of flies. You do not become emotionally involved with flies. Fortunately for humanity, and unfortunately for research in learning, all of us are intimately involved with our fellow men. Therefore, research and theorizing concerning the beautiful, delicate, unbelievably complex, and uniquely human process called *learning* is barely above the "fly level" of research operation described above.

What Is Known about Learning

It is known that conditions can be arranged so that a man can expose himself, or be exposed, to information or a habit (skill or preference) so that the man can reproduce the information or habit at some future time. It is known that learner self arrangement, or teacher arrangement of the conditions of learning are best made when the principles of readiness, motivation, involvement, primacy, exercise, and reinforcement are followed (see Chapter 1). All of this is known as much through the practice of the teaching art, as through the exercise of modern science, for the same principles can be easily gleaned from the seventeenth century writings of Bishop Comenius. Some teachers claim the principles are contained in the ancient Torah.

What does our science know of the psychophysical processes involved in changing a learner from he who does not know (some thing), to he who does know (some thing)? Modern science knows nothing. Scientists and philosophers have some very clever ·guesses—not theories, guesses—as to the specifics of learning, but aside from these guesses, professional educators are no closer to a detailed understanding of the teaching art than were the pedagogues under Comenius' direction.

It is the purpose of this chapter to caution modern professionals to avoid being prejudiced by a certain school of guesses as to the learning process, and to urge modern educators to evaluate instructional approaches on their applicability to the task at hand. Many teachers are influenced more than they realize by one school or another of "learning theory," not because they have been overly exposed to the details of a theory, but because they have been proselytized by proponents of a "theory." These learning notions are from time to time proselytized by program writers, college teachers, popular writers, administrators, and practicing public school educators. Such proselytizing may have already prejudiced many professionals to operate on the "fly level" of objectivity. It behooves all professionals to rise above the fly level, to resist the objectivity dulling influences of social and professional pressures. It is the task of professionals to resist the Zeitgeist (current popular pressure), and to choose learning strategies appropriate to the demands of specific learners, specific curricular goals, and specific teacher personalities. In this chore, teachers can gain much assistance from scientific notions or views of the learning process, so long as teachers avoid becoming disciples to one particular view. An eclectic approach of picking and choosing the description of learning that best fits the learner, the curriculum, and the teacher of the moment can provide guidance, insight, and professional justification for what you do in your classroom tomorrow.

The specifics of the learning process are as numerous as the proponents of individual notions, and each proponent has, or thinks he has, a unique description of what learning is. Rather than list several dozen of these descriptions, we have chosen to categorize the prevalent notions into four broad categories. The categories are: (1) The Rat-in-Maze View; (2) The Data Processing View; (3) The Wildflower View; and (4) The Linguistics View. Test your objectivity by finding some clues to improving your own teaching from each of the views, and by your avoidance of accepting the exclusive efficacy of any single view of learning.

Understand Rat-in-Maze Learning

The Rat-in-Maze view of learning has been defended as the only truly "scientific" view of the learning process. Indeed, a decade ago, the view was synonomous with "learning theory."

You may recall psychology texts showing a little box representing the learner, an arrow pointing to the box and representing learner stimulation, and an arrow emanating from the box representing learner action. All sorts of mechanistic devices were supposed to be inside of the box to represent things happening inside of the learner's skull. The Rat-Maze proponents made extensive use of small animals to test their hypotheses, and to support various arguments about the little boxes inside of the basic box drawn to represent the learner.

Rat-Maze proponents insist that learning progress in basic, ordered steps in a linear manner from simple to complex. Most proponents defend the material reward for learner completion of each ordered step as a necessary contributor to efficient learning.

Many makers of programmed learning devices and teaching machines rely heavily upon the Rat-Maze view, even going so far as to offer the young learner an "M and M" or raisin for each correct response to a request for behavior. A few secondary school teachers have carried the idea to the high school by offering their learners Green Stamp rewards for proper responses to carefully graded learning tasks.

There is a tendency for Rat-Maze people to look upon the thinking ability of human learners as irrelevant to the learning task. Sometimes this is true. Certainly, there is little thought involved in manipulating the levers of a piece of machinery, such as an automobile or typewriter, and Rat-Maze devices are most effective in conditioning individuals to perform such tasks. Similarly, the acquisition of a basic idiomatic vocabulary in a foreign language appears to be suited to techniques which have come from the Rat-Maze viewpoint. Conversely, the mechanical aspects of what you are now doing, reading, would appear to be suited to Rat-Maze techniques, since you are hopefully thinking about what you are reading, rather than consciously aware of the skills you are bringing to the process of reading. However, Rat-Maze techniques have not proved to be superior (or inferior) to other techniques in teaching beginning reading, although they are effective in increasing the reading rate of accomplished readers. Rat-Maze techniques are not at all suited to providing pupils with the cultural understandings and appreciations which are often the advanced and ultimate goals of foreign language instruction.

Learner styles cannot be ignored. While most children will respond to techniques generated by the Rat-Maze view when these techniques are appropriate to the learning task, some children will not respond. Lab researchers destroy rats that refuse to behave like normal rats in the learning situations. Indeed, lab researchers have been criticized for an eugenic error in allowing only for survival of the "learningest" thereby making their lab populations so different from the normal rat that they are now operating with an animal more machinelike than ratlike. That's their problem. Your problem is that you are prohibited by your conscience and society from destroying your non-responders. If your learners refuse to respond to techniques emanating from the Rat-in-Maze view of learning, then you need to take another view of learning.

Understand Data Processing Learning

Another view of learning, the Data Processing View, has developed as a result of the alleged similarities between modern automatic data processing machines, particularly computers, and the human nervous system. This is not to say that cognitive psychologists believe either that computers are capable of original thinking, or that people are not capable of original thinking. It is to say that some cognitive psychologists see the computer circuitry as a crude, but handy, model for describing human memory and problem solving ability.

An example will illustrate. Professor Anokhin of the Moscow (USSR) Sechenov Institute is a leading proponent of the Data Processing View. The view holds that human cognition is composed of three major systems: (1) data input; (2) data storage or memory; and (3) retrieval or performance.

According to Anokhin's model, learner perception (sight, hearing, etc.) is the data input to the human data processing system. The data to be retained are stored as "bits" of information represented by nucleic acid chains within brain cells. Irrelevant "bits" are erased chemically, "bits" to be retained are lodged in the cells as acid chains. Data processing (thinking) and retrieval (performance) are accomplished through complex electrochemical processes (programs) resulting from both the influence of drives and conditioning.

The Data Processing view of learning is more sophisticated than the Rat-Maze view. It allows for thinking on the part of learners, for learning resulting from intuitive leaps as well as from carefully built stimulus-response patterns, and for application of stored information or habit patterns to apparently unique performance chores.

Many learning materials which aim to build basic thinking and acting strategies applicable to a wide variety of similar tasks appeal to the Data Processing view researchers for support. Most of the so called "new math" programs fall into this category, as do programs pointed toward building broadly applicable study skills beyond the basic skills of reading decoding. Some of the widely advertised private tutors of memory skills base their instruction upon the Data Processing view that human storage and retrieval of information is optimized by training learners to categorize information in meaningful, or even artificial, mnemonic structures to insure effective information retrieval. This is hardly a new idea, but the Data Processing view does lend some support to the idea that organized (categorized) facts or concepts are better retained and used by learners than are unorganized or unrelated facts or concepts.

Both the Rat-Maze and the Data Processing views of learning provide support and guidance for professionals who need techniques to aid learners in achieving the academic learning objectives discussed in Chapter 4. There is less help from these views for teachers involved in leading learners to achieve other kinds of objectives. When dealing with other kinds of objectives, it is necessary to take a view of learning different from either the Rat-Maze or Data Processing view.

Understand the Wildflower View

The Wildflower view of learning is different from the views mentioned above. Within this school there are no formal notions of how learning takes place; there are no little boxes pierced by arrows; and no instances of gleaming computer circuitry. There is only the very beautiful belief that humans are individually unique, unpredictable, fragile, and above cognitive classification. Rousseau's *Emile* is a statement of a Wildflower view.

Modern proponents of the Wildflower view hold that for human learning to take place, the thing to be learned must be: (1) chosen by the learner; (2) intensely interesting to the learner; and (3) somehow capable of application to a real-life pursuit that the learner wishes to undertake immediately.

The Wildflower view has provided educators with some valuable concepts concerning readiness for learning, motivation, and the recognition of individual differences. Creators of learning materials which allow for even a restricted learner choice of learning tasks have been influenced by the Wildflower view, as have creators of materials designed to aid learners in self-discovery of certain discriminations and generalizations.

We disagree with certain hard nosed proponents of the Wildflower view who criticize professionals for engaging in the planning of learning activities. Planning is essential to the reasonable and defensible direction of any human activity, including highly creative activities. The act of planning does not erase the possibility of serendipitous occurrences; indeed, planning may result in valuable accidents. The catch to the above paradox is to avoid being made rigid by plans. As long as the plans described in earlier chapters are treated as flexible guides to the conduct of learning activities, and not as stone-inscribed commands from Mount Sinai, you can have both the direction and continuity provided by plans, and the "happy accidents" provided by chance. However, when chance fails to operate in positive ways to promote learning, which is most of the time, the plans are available to provide positive guidance.

The Wildflower view does provide an approach valuable in the building of attitudes and values in learners. In this pursuit, the techniques of providing emulatable peer and adult models, and the provision of enjoyable activities serve better in achieving the desired learner behaviors than do more formal and direct means of instruction.

As recently as five years ago, this chapter would have presented only the Rat-Maze, Data Processing, and Wildflower views of learning. Now, a fourth view of learning, which we call the Linguistics view occupies the efforts of a growing number of cognitive psychologists. The Linguistics view has contributed two major learning concepts pregnant with potential applications possibilities.

Understand the Linguistics Approach to Learning

The term *linguistics* is not only the title of a type of scientific study of language. Researchers in psycholinguistics have developed sophisticated ideas of how learning takes place. This movement has advanced to the point where Chomsky, the linguist, has proved himself capable of carrying on a serious academic debate on thought process with Skinner, the psychologist.

One valuable prescription for learning attributable to the Linguistics view of learning is that instructors ground pupils in a knowledge of the real world before attempting to teach learners to discriminate among, or generalize from abstractions of things or ideas.

An example will illustrate. Most programs for beginning readers attempt to present young children with easily-read descriptions of objects and events familiar to most young children. This is an attempt by publishers and authors to recognize a Linguistics view principle, and have young learners abstract from what they know of the real world to print and picture. Nevertheless, you have observed reading teachers (or other teachers) attempting to build a concept of a *tractor* for a city child who has never seen a tractor, or an *apartment* for a rural child who has never seen an apartment, from print or picture descriptions in the readers. This, say the linguists, is asking the child to abstract from abstractions, and results in the meaningless mouthing of verbiage instead of the desired reading for meaning. The Linguistics view lends support to the seemingly endless "field trips" provided in many pre-school programs, and in some elementary and secondary school programs.

It is impossible to totally avoid asking learners to abstract from abstractions. School resources preclude showing learners all of the seeable objects in the real world, and some concepts that we teach are abstract to the degree that they have no grounding in reality. Nevertheless, the Linguistics view does aid teachers in: (1) cautioning them to avoid abstracting from abstractions whenever the practice is unnecessary to the learning task at hand; (2) prescribing that they attempt to ground an abstraction in reality by showing learners the real thing; and (3) alerting teachers to recognize and prepare for the learning problems of students required to achieve a grasp of ungrounded abstractions.

The second principle provided by the Linguistics view is that learning and retention are maximized when the thing to be learned is presented and practiced in a meaningful conceptual structure. Naturally, the common linguistics example of this principle involves language. Try to memorize the following six words:

gatchins
nilly
very
require
Zoffs
all

Now that you have memorized the words, how long do you think that you will remember them? Probably not beyond the next five minutes. Rat-Maze people would say that you have not had enough repetitions of the memory exercise to support long term recall. Data Processing people would say that the neucleic acid chains (or other chemical representative) were "erased" or buried from retrieval due to the obvious irrelevancy of the list to any conceivable use. Wildflower view people would not have memorized the list in the first place, since no real reason was provided for memorizing the list. Linguistics view people would say you forgot, or will soon forget, the list because (1) three list words are not tied to anything existing in the real world, and (2) the words fit no language structure with which you are familiar. That is, they fit no structure unless you structured them yourself for more efficient recall.

The same words would be easier to recall and memorize if placed in a familiar language structure such as:

All Zoffs require very nilly gatchins.

Within the familiar language structure (admittedly a "surface structure") the six words are easy to recall, and even without the vaguest idea of what the sentence means you can answer questions such as:

What do Zoffs require?
What type of gatchins do Zoffs require?

Note how your recall of the six words is aided by the familiar sentence structure. Also, you correctly answered that Zoffs require gatchins, and that the gatchins were of the very nilly type. Your recall was aided by the structure of the six word sentence, and your ability to abstract from the nonsense abstraction was demonstrated.

Language building programs which strive to train learners to use specific language patterns are utilizing the Linguistics view of learning. The pattern giving aspects of the view are contrary to a school which holds that patterns or structures are best learned by discovery. The final judgment is yours. How did you learn the six word list as first presented; Did you simply memorize the list, as given? If so, your learning style was not oriented toward structure-finding for the list memorizing task. Did you attempt to order the list in some structure, such as arranging the words in alphabetical order? If so, your learning style for the task' was geared to a mnemonic popular among Data Processing people. Finally, if you saw the possibility of organizing the list in a familiar language pattern, then you were a discovery learner for the task.

Take the Eclectic Approach to Learning

Rat-Maze views of learning, Data Processing views of learning, Wildflower views of learning, and Linguistics views of learning are all attempts to describe *the* process of learning. None do. However, all provide a way to approach learners, and a way to organize, or not organize, learning experiences.

Until *the* theory of learning has been successfully defended, all that the teacher can do is remain an objective observer of all views of learning, the thing to be learned, the learner, and himself. You can bring your professional skills and experience to focus upon diagnosing each specific learning situation, and choosing the view of learning that will aid you in prescribing the proper learning activities suited to the learning task, the learner, and to you. Expect that you as typing teacher will view learning very differently from you as fine arts teacher. Furthermore, you as English teacher will view learning differently when the object of instruction is proper punctuation than when the object of instruction is poetry appreciation.

This is an eclectic approach to learning process, and the only sensible approach for the practicing instructor.

10

Take a New View
of Teaching Methods

Speaking of Methods

Your college instructor talked about "teaching methods." Lots of books talk about "methods." We talk to each other about "methods." No one is very specific about what "methods" are. Are there really such things as "teaching methods?" Yes, there are, and it is high time for specificity.

Let's be specific. Professor Kelly Duncan of the Ohio State University has analyzed the work of hundreds of experienced teachers in action, and he has distinguished four basic methods for communicating information from teacher to learner. Just four.

These methods of instruction are *direct communication, teacher-student discussion, independent student activity,* and *group student activity.* That's all. Look at the methods individually.

I. USE DIRECT COMMUNICATION

Direct Communication is the only information passing method available to the people who write programs for television. It's the only method available to people who write books. Direct communication is the teaching method used by you when you deliver a lecture to others.

A good deal of nonsense has been written and said about the ineffectiveness of direct communication in classrooms. Direct

communication is neither good, nor bad. Like any communications tool, it simply *is*. The goodness or badness of the tool is
determined by how you use it, and what you use it for.

Obviously, lecture is a poor method for teaching reading in
elementary school, and it has limited use in a physics lab in high
school. A physical education teacher would look silly if he spent
an entire semester delivering lectures to his students on the correct :
method for playing football. People improve their reading by
reading, their ability to use lab equipment by using lab equipment,
and their ability to play football by playing football.

Conversely, lecture is a good method for building the *familiarity*
with a new subject field as discussed in previous chapters. Lecture
can also build upon familiarity to develop the knowledge level of
learning. Every experienced history or social studies teacher knows
it is folly to expect students to intelligently discuss, or work
independently with material the students know nothing about.

A personal example with illustrate. Sam Hudson, a very new
teacher in a Philadelphia middle school was asked to substitute
during one period for a seventh-grade art teacher. Sam bounded
into the class armed with zero art teaching experience, and a large
baggage of theory acquired from his teacher training courses. Most
of his baggage consisted of "don'ts." Don't inhibit the pupil's
creativity. Don't criticize a student's honest expression. Don't
change anything on a student's paper. The only thing that Sam
was supposed to do was be in the classroom.

The absent teacher's plan directed Sam to teach the children
something about symmetrical design. What about symmetrical
design was unclear, and the absent teacher's mistake. What Sam
did was his mistake.

Sam's instruction to the class was admirable, according to the
theory of the time. He told students to take brush and paper, and
to make a symmetrical design. Sam didn't violate a single "don't."

The results were a disaster. Of course, the students did not
know what they were to do. True to what Sam had been taught,
he kept his peace as students messed with paint and paper
throughout the period, and true to what he had been taught, Sam
displayed all of the resultant "creations" on the classroom wall.

When the regular art teacher returned he patiently listened to
Sam's proud explanations of the many "don'ts" he had avoided,

and to Sam's disappointment at the abominable results. "Why," asked Sam, "didn't the creative ability of these pupils come forward under my non-restrictive approach?"

The art teacher's retort was classic. He looked Sam square in the eye and replied, "You have to teach them something first."

By "teach" he meant directly communicate. Directly communicate either through lecture, through use of models, through use of motion picture media or television, or through a combination of sensual stimulations. By "teach" he meant build pupil familiarity, knowledge, and understanding of the process before expecting application.

When You Use Direct Communication

Use of direct communication is dictated by the level of learning you are aiming for. Direct communication is your only approach to the achievement of goals at the *familiarity* level of learning. It is also a useful approach to the achievement of goals at the *knowledge* level of learning. Direct communication is not usually appropriate to the achievement of goals at the *understanding* or *application* levels of learning.[1]

An example will illustrate. Do you find the annual back-to-school-night-for-parents meeting a dreaded chore? How about that half-hour or so when you are expected to entertain the parents in your classroom? Is it an informative half-hour? Or is it a traumatic experience as parents ask worse than superficial questions, and squirm in their seats through long periods of silence while you try to stimulate discussion? For most teachers the situation is not pleasant because teachers are asking parents to respond at a level of learning appropriate to an understanding of the classroom goals and procedures, while the parents have no familiarity or knowledge about what is going on. Familiarity and knowledge must be built through direct communication.

Try this at your next back-to-school-night. Prepare a short ten minute lecture highlighting (not detailing) what you intend to teach, how you intend to teach it, and why you intend to teach it. Keep your presentation simple, and don't be afraid of boring

---

[1] See page 20 for a review of the four levels of learning.

parents with information that seems obvious to you. Parents avoid asking questions at these sessions because nothing of what goes on in schools is obvious to them. They have no familiarity with the art of teaching.

After you have familiarized parents with your program through direct communication, then give them a chance to ask questions. You will be amazed at the flood of questions, and at the quality of questions that you receive. Use this technique, and that half-hour that used to seem endless will fly by in a blur.

The moral of this story is that you use direct communication as the initiating spark satisfying familiarity and knowledge building goals so you can successfully move to other methods to meet understanding and application goals. This holds true for teaching children, teachers, parents, anyone.

Direct Communication Makes Sense

Professional teachers have a number of direct communication tools from which to choose. Lecture is most readily available, and most misused. In addition to lecture, there is the directed reading assignment, motion pictures and television, filmstrips and slides, programmed learning materials, and computer assisted instructional devices.

Lecture is the most maligned of all teaching methods in the professional literature, and yet according to research with the Flanders Instrument,[2] lecture is what teachers do most of. Lecture has been criticized as boring, futile, and inappropriate to instruction.

Boring? Between thirty and fifty million people voluntarily tune to NBC or CBS every evening to hear David Brinkley or Walter Cronkite moderate a series of little lectures.

Futile? The producers of CBS and NBC programming bet a great deal of cash that their lectures will attract people to watch the news programs. The sponsors of the programs bet more cash that the little lectures they interspace throughout the programs will teach people to buy their products.

Inappropriate? Lecture is not inappropriate to sellers of pharmaceuticals who wish to familiarize television viewers with the

---

[2]See Chapter 11 for a discussion of this tool.

virtues of their products, or to sellers of credit as they familiarize viewers with their services.

Patent medicine and credit sellers have been singled out as the sponsors who most frequently use lecture to introduce new products totally unfamiliar to potential buyers. Drug and credit sellers first familiarize their publics *via* lectures, and only after this familiarization step do they move into direct communication through non-lecture vehicles such as dramatizations or artistic exhibitions of their products. Watch this process.

Inappropriate to instruction? Socrates didn't find lecture inappropriate, nor did Mark Hopkins. Russell Conwell's *Acres of Diamonds* lecture moved and taught tens of thousands—one lecture. Evangelists from St. Paul to Billy Graham have effectivly taught their own brand of history and philosophy through lecture. Lecture is not inappropriate to instruction; nevertheless, inappropriate lectures scuttle instruction.

How to Plan a Decent Lecture

Classroom lectures are most appropriate to meeting familiarization and understanding level instructional goals. For this reason, you plan classroom lectures to answer (or raise) six basic questions: the who, what, when, where, why, and how of whatever you are teaching.

In answering, or raising, the six basic questions through lecture, you must remember that you are not supplying in-depth answers. You are merely building familiarity or understanding. Lectures, especially classroom lectures, must be kept uncomplicated to be effective.

Simplicity must be stressed. The literature of educational physchology clearly directs that any lecture, regardless of length, must make three or less major points. The assimilation of three major points is the limit of listener retention. Limitation of lectures to two, or even one point reduces cognitive strain on the part of the listener, and increases the impact of what is being communicated.

The major point, or points, of the lecture must be developed through use of analogies, personal stories, examples, expositions, explanations, demonstrations, witticisms, homilies, parables, discriminations, and/or generalizations. How many of these communciations devices you use, and which of them you choose depends upon your personality. Let's look at the pros. Harry Reasoner relies heavily upon carefully chosen examples to clearly illustrate the one bold point to which he usually limits his T.V. essays. Russell Conwell relied almost solely upon the personal story to transfix his listeners, and hammer home his point. William Buckley drives home his customary two or three points per lecture through skillful use of logical explanations, analogies, witticisms, and examples.

The illustration in Figure 10-1 shows that 95 percent of your lecture is going to be devoted to background material. The background is designed to illustrate, enliven, or reify the point you are trying to make, to familiarize the learner with new material, or to build new understandings upon his familiarity with a subject. Furthermore, the point is chained to the learner by the learner's familiarity with the context material. Reasoner's examples are always familiar examples, Conwell's personal stories were easily followed by his listeners, and Buckley develops his explanations and analogies from the most familiar of premises and events. These men exemplify mastery of the art of attaching the point to learners through the use of familiar contexts.

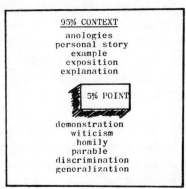

Figure 10-1. Make the Point of Your Lecture Stand Out.

After you have planned a lecture, review it to insure you:

1. stress three or less main points . . . . ☐
2. answer two or more of the six basic questions . . . . ☐
3. utilize lecture primarily to achieve "familiarity" or "understanding" goals . . . . ☐

4. attach your point to the learners by using a familiar context . . . . ☐
5. consciously choose communications devices to suit your personality . . . . ☐
6. carve the point you are making in bold relief against the contextual background of the lecture . . . . ☐

When you can deliver a "yes" answer to all six questions, you are ready to utilize lecture as an effective means of direct communication.

II. USE TEACHER-STUDENT INTERACTION

Teacher-student interaction is not available to big-time lecturers, or to T.V. programmers. This means of involving learners is only available to people like us who deal with groups of ten or thirty or fifty people. The circuit lecturers and entertainers wish they could get interactive involvement with their thousand plus audiences. Media "talk shows" and lecture hall question and answer sessions; letters to editors and open phone lines to broadcasters have been mildly successful in achieving a low degree of audience interactive involvement with the speaker. In the final analysis, the meeters of mass audiences have an edge on those of us who must prepare and transmit different information every day to teachers and students. They have the time and resources to build all sorts of clever lectures illustrated by slick visuals and motion pictures. However, we have the edge on the mass media when it comes to the teacher-student interaction method of teaching. We usually work with groups of about thirty pupils, and we can sub-group to get smaller audiences when desirable. Teacher-student interaction is where we excell—or should excell. We can *get* interaction.

You can get interaction, but you cannot get it automatically. Oh, you can get a student to mutter sounds by telling him to turn to page 78 and read the second paragraph aloud, but that is not interaction. That is concert reading practice. Teacher-student interaction is a two-way conversation between teacher and pupil in which both teacher and pupil are involved—involved in organizing, talking, thinking, and learning.

Interaction is fairly easy to achieve when just you and one pupil converse. Interaction becomes a high art when it is necessary to simultaneously involve ten or thirty or fifty pupils and the teacher in a single conversation. Interaction on that level is a high art, but one successfully practiced by hundreds of excellent teachers every day.

There are two parts to successful classroom interaction. These are getting it, and keeping it. Let's get it first.

Getting Interaction

Within the direct communication section a back-to-school-night session was described. The situation pictured a teacher expecting to stimulate interaction by simply requesting parent questions. The teacher got silence.

You don't get interaction by asking for it. You get interaction by setting conditions so that it is impossible for listeners *not* to interact.

The first step in setting these conditions is to do a little furniture arranging. That's right, furniture arranging. The Group Dynamics people are agreed that furniture arrangement has a good deal to do with whether or not interaction takes place at all, and that the placement of the chairs has something to do with the type of interaction that takes place.

The desk arrangements diagrams will be used to illustrate. The "A" situation in Figure 10-2 is the traditional lecture arrangement of teacher facing long rows of students. This arrangement is not conducive to interaction.

The "A" situation can be quickly changed to the "B" situation where the teacher is physically able to see and be seen by all of the pupils.

The "A" situation can also be changed to the "C" situation which places the teacher nearest to the most pupils. Either "B" or "C" will be more conducive to teacher-student interaction than will "A".

Arrangement "D" is superior to all of the other furniture arrangements if some pupil-pupil interaction is desired.

The big moral of the furniture arrangement story is that all pupils should have a clear line of sight to the teacher, and that the most complete interaction results when the pupils have a clear line of sight to each other as well.

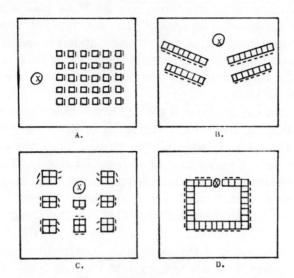

Figure 10-2. Desk Arrangements Help Interaction.

The second step in getting interaction is to insure that learners are familiar with the material they are supposed to be using in the interaction situation. As stated above, the familiarity level of learning is achieved through some means of direct communication such as viewing a movie, listening to lecture, or reading some print (silently, like real people read). Teacher-pupil interaction is a method for raising familiarity to understanding, understanding to knowledge, or knowledge to application. Learners must know something before they can talk about it.

Given proper furniture arrangement, and students who have at least a familiarity with the subject does not guarantee interaction. If you haven't been faced by thirty "bumps on a log" at some time when you wanted a class discussion, Don Bailey has. Don Bailey is the science coordinator for the Middleburg Public Schools. Here's what happened.

Don was called in to a sixth-grade science class to teach an eight week demonstration unit centered upon the solar system. The curriculum guide specified that he build in learners a familiarity with major theories from Ptolemy to Newton, and a knowledge of the "geography" of the solar system.

Don Bailey knew that the children he would teach had been

previously exposed to the "turn to page 75 of your science text and read paragraph two aloud" concert reading approach to science instruction. As a result, the pupils viewed their daily science period with a feeling more appropriate to a trip to the dentist than to a stimulating learning experience. They expected the same from Don.

On the first day of the unit the children sat silently with science texts dutifully turned to the first page of the solar system unit. Knowing that it is a rare sixth-grader who does not have some familiarity with the arrangement of the solar system, Don politely told the children to put their books away. The children were puzzled, but not ready to discuss what they knew of the subject.

The furniture arrangement was O.K. so Don began with an interaction getting lecture. His single point for the first thirty minute lecture was that the earth is the center of the solar system and the universe. Don did not say that Ptolemy *thought* that the earth was the center. He taught that modern science has *proved* that the earth is the center. A couple of the more astute pupils looked as if they doubted Don's mastery of the subject, but they were not ready to say anything on the first day.

In subsequent lectures on days that followed, Don developed more of his bastardized Ptolemaic theory, assuring children that the information was valid, and of recent vintage. The deeper he got into descriptions of stationary earth, plexiglass globes supporting sun, moon, and planets, Martian proximity to Venus, and planetary epicycles on railroad tracks, the more looks of horror and indignation registered on the children's faces. Finally, on the fifth day, one dear girl looked at Don with what can only be descirbed as rage, and without the customary hand-raising blurted, "Mr. Bailey, the next thing you'll be telling us is that the world is flat!"

With deadpan expression Don assured her that recent evidence indicated that the world *is* flat. He invited her to look out of the window at the world to verify this.

Following the flat earth remark, there was extensive teacher-student interaction. Even before the girl's explosion, Don had observed children sneaking peeks at the science texts he had prohibited them from reading, but after the flat earth statement there was open appeal to the texts to refute his arguments for a Ptolemaic solar system. There was also interaction.

Only a motivational stunt, you say? Sure. But one that you can use to get interaction. Try it. Describe an adjective as a noun sometime, teach the fact that Pennsylvania is on the West Coast of the U.S. and prove it by holding the map to the window to project a reverse image, teach the Phlogiston Theory as a "latest" scientific discovery, or teach your foreign language pupils that people of another culture behave in an outlandish way that your students know is unlikely.

This "shock treatment" is the surest way to set conditions so that interaction is not only likely to result, but that it is impossible for students *not* to react to you, and interact with you.

We recognize that the "shock" approach to getting interaction could be construed to violate the law of primacy discussed in Chapter 1. To be effective, the technique requires that the teacher present information that goes counter to something with which pupils are at least familiar already. Primacy is what makes the technique shock pupils. Of course the technique must be limited to outlandish performances, such as Don Bailey engineered, and the technique will grow stale if overused.

We also recognize that the "shock" approach may upset some parents. Don Bailey expected to receive some parent calls protesting his "misguiding" of the children. He was prepared to explain his instructional approach to concerned parents, and he was successful in doing this to the two (out of thirty-four) upset mothers who called him.

Maintaining Interaction

Pupil-teacher interaction is a two-way street. You can force students to react to you once or twice, but what follows depends upon how you react to their reaction. This *is* interaction.

Four factors stand out to make or break on-going teacher-student interaction. These factors are *group size, teacher remarks, teacher non-verbal behavior,* and *pupil behavior.*

Group Size Affects Interaction

Obviously, as group size is decreased, interaction is easier to maintain. This is true down to a five member group. Our own research[3] showed less interaction as the group member numbers dropped below five. Try for an instructional group of between five and thirty or so pupils. Whenever you want intensive interaction, divide an average size class in half, and promote interaction with a group of about fifteen pupils. You will need to experiment to find out what works for you.

Teacher Replies Affect Interaction

Your replies to pupil remarks constitute the second determiner of whether or not interaction takes place. It is easy to cut a child off with a response to his participation such as one of the following:

Interaction Inhibiting
Remarks
I.

Teacher: "What is this thing we call a *plateau?*"
Pupil: "A hill with a flat top."
Teacher: "Yes, a hill with a flat top."

II.

Teacher: "What is this thing we call a *plateau?*"
Pupil: "A hill with a flat top."
Teacher: "Good. How about a *mountain?* What's that?"

III.

Teacher: "What is this thing we call a *plateau?*"
Pupil: "It's a mountain, made of ice."
Teacher: "No!" That's a *glacier.* What's the matter with you? Didn't you read your book?"

It is also possible to maximize interaction with a response such as the following:

Interaction Encouraging
Remarks
IV.

Teacher: "What is this thing we call a *plateau?*"
Pupil: "A hill with a flat top."
Teacher: "Good. Tell me more."

V.

Teacher: "What is this thing we call a *plateau?*"
Pupil: "A hill with a flat top."
Teacher: "Uh-huh. Go on."

---

[3]Charles Christine and Dorothy W. Christine. "The Influence of Group Member Number Upon the Problem Solving Ability of the Group," *Journal of Psychological Studies.* 14:172-176, Dec. 1963.

VI.

Teacher: "What is this thing we call a *plateau?*"
Pupil: "It's a mountain, made of ice."
Teacher: "Would you double check that in your textbook? I'll come
           back to you in a minute." (Skips to next topic.)

In situation *I* the teacher will get response, but not interaction. Once established, the question-answer-teacher repeats answer-new question pattern goes on for many lessons. Situation II is almost the same as *I.* Establishing such a pattern as II will force the teacher to jump from topic to topic without really developing much beyond a familiarity with concepts, which we presume the children began with anyway. Furthermore, pupils will be too exhausted trying to keep up to do any interacting. Interaction takes time. Situation III will make many pupils wary of giving *any* response. No one likes to be embarrassed and criticized in front of others.

In situations IV and V the teacher is non-directive in encouraging pupils to develop their reporting and thinking to the fullest extent possible. Following these situations pupils will begin to realize that more than a simple one-word or one-sentence answer is expected and appreciated. Situation VI is one way of indicating an incorrect response without unduly embarrassing the pupil. In VI the teacher does not call upon one of the other ten children who are wildly waving their hands to answer. Instead, the teacher gives the pupil an opportunity to re-check a source at leisure, and to report correctly later. The leisure is provided by the teacher's occupying the rest of the class with another topic, and returning to the plateau topic later when it is obvious the pupil who answered incorrectly now has the proper information. Do this, and the "silent pupils" will learn that you will not step on their egos should they falter. Do this, and watch silent pupils become participating pupils.

The teacher comments and interaction discussed here are designed to give you a broad view of the teacher-student interaction method. More specific information is provided in Chapter 11 of this book.

Teacher Non-Verbal Behavior Affects Interaction

What you say is only part of what you *communicate* to pupils. Your facial expressions, eye contact, and gestures carry powerful messages, For example, the effect of teacher words in situation VI could be negated if said with a look of disgust, if said with the teacher's back to the pupil, or if said as the teacher's arms were lowered and breath exhaled in the classic gesture of teacher disappointment and defeat.

Your non-verbal communications are a good deal more difficult to control than the verbal ones; however, non-verbal communications can be controlled. You can control them.

Start with eye contact. When a pupil is speaking, look at him. Keep looking at him. We all gauge our listener's attention by the amount of time he spends looking at us, and pupils are no different. Look and really listen.

Control the look of disgust. Sure, pupils will come up with bloopers at times. We all make mistakes, that's why erasers are on pencils. Practice discarding the how-can-he-say-that-when-I've-told-him-otherwise look, and substitute the puzzled expression to accompany the teacher remark in situation VI. It will pay off in improved pupil responses.

Pupil Remarks Affect Interaction

To maintain a high level of classroom interaction, it is necessary to maintain good pupil-pupil interaction as well as good teacher-student interaction. What have you observed that a happening such as situation VII does in your classroom?

VII.

Teacher: "Very good. You do punctuate a subordinate clause with a comma. Tell me more about subordinate clauses."
Pupil: (in a serious manner) "Well, they all modify a noun."
Classmates: Wild laughter.

It is easy to predict that the pupil will not speak up in class for quite a while.

Preventing occurrences such as situation VII is vital to your classroom interaction, and you can prevent such occurrences. An honest interaction situation must be carefully built, and the building necessitates teacher lectures, and teacher-student discussions of the requirement for respecting the feelings of all class members.

An example of how this respect can be taught was provided

when we observed Mr. Kane. Mr. Kane was a high school math teacher who had taken the extra assignment of teaching an evening business arithmetic course to adults in the community. During the first hour that the class met, Mr. Kane announced his intention to devote his first unit to various types of credit devices, and methods of calculating their costs. He first asked the class if there was anyone present who could not compute simple interest.

One lonely hand was raised, and many of the men in the class began to snicker. The face attached to the hand began to turn red.

Mr. Kane, without a blink, launched into a long congratulation of the man who "had the courage" to admit his limitation. He continued with a generalized lecture which has the single point of extolling those who were aware of their limitations, and were willing to admit limitations in a world that laughs at such people.

What did Kane do wrong? Had he phrased his initial question to read, "Is there anyone in the class who *can* compute simple interest?" he would have avoided the obviousness of two or three brave souls standing out in the group in a negative fashion.

What did Kane do right? Mr. Kane spent fifteen minutes of his first class meeting setting an atmosphere where teacher-student interaction was possible. During the next eighteen weeks he got participation from, and interaction with his students. The man who had been laughed at did not drop out of the class, but gained a tremendous respect and trust in Mr. Kane, and the embarrassed man did participate in future discussions.

Reprise

Teacher-student interaction does not just happen. You must build interaction, and through your control of group size, teacher comments, teacher actions, and pupil behavior you must maintain it.

III. USE INDEPENDENT STUDENT ACTIVITY

Independent student activity is used to achieve the higher levels of learning—understanding and application. In a way, the method of independent student activity *is* the student's application of knowledge and understanding to a particular project.

Two important principles determine whether or not independent student activity is usable in a given situation. First, independent activity can only be utilized by learners who are *at least* at the knowledge level of learning. Second, pupils must want to engage in the activity. Two examples will illustrate.

The Kindergarten Example

The children were engaged in their daily "free activity" period. Some children messed with paints, some engaged in dramatic play, some played with blocks. Mrs. Lake observed Tony as he played alone with a small "number balance." The number balance is a small balance arm upon which can be hung two-inch high weighted plastic numerals (Figure 10-3). The numerals are weighted so that the arm will center whenever identical numerals, or numeral sums, are represented on opposite arms of the balance beam. Tony was simply trying to hang all of the plastic numerals on one balance arm in a random fashion.

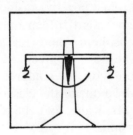

Figure 10-3. The Number Balance.

Mrs. Lake quietly sat down next to Tony. Without saying a word she cleared the numerals from the balance arm. Next, she hung a plastic "two" on the left arm, and the left arm descended. Following this, she hung another plastic "two" on the right arm, and the scale balanced. Tony watched with great interest.

Mrs. Lake continued to balance various numerals while Tony watched. Without ever having said a word to Tony, she left the table, and retreated to a far corner of the room. Tony resumed control of the number balance, and began to ape what his teacher had done, balancing three against three, six against six. After five minutes of this activity, Tony forgot to clear a plastic "three" from the left arm. He hung a plastic "one" on the left arm, and a plastic "one" one the right arm. The beam still tilted to the left. Tony rechecked the arms in a puzzled manner, and discovered the two numerals on the left arm. In a flash he added a plastic "three" to the right arm, and restored the balance. He then cleared the number balance, and proceeded to balance two numerals on each arm instead of the previously used one numeral per arm. Tony had taken a beginning step in developing a concept of numeral equality through an independent student activity.

The High School Example

Mr. Art is a high school English teacher, and a good one. We visited his class to observe his techniques for teaching a homogeneous senior English class, a bad one. The students were, for the most part, boys on the thinnest verge of becoming drop-outs.

The curriculum guide dictated that part of Mr. Art's job was to lead his pupils to read, understand, and appreciate Poe's *The Gold Bug*. Art, a skillful oral reader, had read part of the novel *to* his pupils for he was certain they couldn't or wouldn't read it for themselves. He had previously read the story aloud to the page where the code is reproduced.

On the day that we visited, Art had reproduced the code page on the overhead, and he was lecturing on the subject of codes and cryptography. Art was able to stimulate considerable interest among the pupils with his lecture background material. The background material contained stories illustrating the seamier sides of military and police code breaking activities. He hammered his two points that codes can be broken, and that code breaking is a manly activity.

The familiarity lecture was followed by a teacher-pupil discussion of code breaking. During the discussion Art didn't miss the opportunity to reinforce a few phonics generalizations when the subject of vowel-consonant relations was broached. Nevertheless, he kept returning the discussion to center on the point of how "manly" this code breaking business can be.

Mr. Art's assignment, given at the end of the discussion, was for the students to decode *The Gold Bug* code on the overhead plate, and in the novel. He watched calmly as three of four of the twenty-two pupils dutifully began to glance at the code page in their books. The other pupils sullenly closed their books in preparation for leaving the class and forgetting the assignment.

Mr. Art was not finished. "Oh yes," he remarked casually, "the first student who brings me the correctly docoded passage tomorrow morning will receive an "A" for the report period. The next five students who reach me with a correctly decoded passage will receive an "A" for the *Gold Bug* project, and the remaining students who hand-in a correct decoding will receive an "A" for the assignment. You must reach me at school tomorrow morning. I will not look at your work if you bring it to me at my home."

We stopped by Mr. Art's office at 8:00 AM the following day. Since school began at 9:00 AM we expected to see some of the action. 8:00 AM was too late. Mr. Art was calmly sitting in his office reading over the last of twenty decodings.

"Couldn't the students have simply read the novel to 'break' the code?" we asked Mr. Art.

Art looked at us with the patient expression he probably reserved for new administrator-specialist teams. "Yes," he answered. "Yes, that would have been the easy way. But, that's what we wanted them to do, isn't it?"

The kindergarten example illustrates a type of independent student activity very close to what has been called the "Discovery Method." Mrs. Lake's intervention to Tony's activity at the number balance, her wordless direct communication of how to use the balance, would be criticized by purists of "discovery" as destroying the child's involvement in discovering the point of the edcuational toy. Tony may have re-invented the principle of the number balance for himself, as demanded by some priests of the Wildflower View, but this is doubtful. However, when he was provided with a familiarity and knowledge of the principle of balances in general, and of the number balance in particular, he was able to quickly move to a level of understanding and crude application through his own activity. The point of independent student activity is to lead the pupil to acquire certain understandings and applications for himself. To make his "discoveries," familiarity and knowledge must be present as the building blocks from which the child's discoveries are constructed. "You have to teach them something first."

Mr. Art had given his pupils a familiarity and knowledge of *The Gold Bug* through his inspired concert readings. He also built a familiarity and knowledge of code breaking during his lecture and teacher-student interaction session. To this careful preparation he added a massive dose of extrinsic motivation to make it nearly impossible for students to avoid engaging in an independent student activity designed to lead some of them to understand Poe's novel, and for some of them to apply their reading skills of skimming and reading for a specific purpose.

How You Can Use Independent Student Activity

You can begin by realizing the two important principles developed above. First, insure that your students have a familiarity with and understanding of the task so they can work *purposefully* on their own. Second, insure that your students have some reason, important to them, for engaging in the independent activity. Tony was intrinsically motivated, Mr. Art's class was moved by the crudest of extrinsic motivations. College professors worry about this. Good teachers use any kind of motivation they can get.

Familiarity and understanding, and motivation begin the process. From there it is up to you to leave the student alone until he either (1) finishes the project, or (2) honestly asks you for help. In the event that a student asks for help before a project is complete, it is your job to clarify his problem for him, but not to solve it for him. As soon as you begin to give the student direct assistance in completing his project, the activity becomes a teacher-pupil interaction situation, and not independent student activity.

You use the technique of independent student activity to help pupils achieve the understanding and application levels of learning. Indeed, independent student activity is the surest method for achieving the application level of learning.

IV. USE GROUP ACTIVITY

The Bus Ride

Think of the last time you rode a public bus. You entered the bus, paid your fare, ignored the other twenty or thirty riders, and minded your own business throughout the trip. You spent many minutes with other people, yet you had nothing to do with any of them. You were with a group, but there was no *group activity*.

Think again of you on the bus. Imagine that the bus ran into a blinding snowstorm, and became stuck in a snowdrift. Naturally, you and the other passengers would feel apprehensive under such circumstances. After all, this is a rather un-buslike event. Naturally, you and the other passengers want to be on your way to your destinations. You want that bus to be unstuck. You and your fellow passengers all want the same thing.

Now you *do* notice your fellow passengers. Now you begin speaking with other passengers in an attempt to reduce anxiety, and to find a way to get out of the drift. You give suggestions as to what can be done, and you listen to suggestions of what to do. This is *group activity*.

What changed? What is different between the collection of people simply riding the bus, and the snowbound group discussing ways to resume their trip? The differences are two. First, the drift-bound people all have a common goal. All wish to resume their trip. Second, the drift-bound group of people is willing to work cooperatively to reach the common goal. A common goal, and the willingness to work cooperatively to reach the goal make group activity possible.

Group Activity and Instruction

Student group activity can be used to meet instructional objectives. Advantages of group activity include:

1. opportunities for greater numbers of pupils to participate in discussions;
2. opportunities for pupils to work with topics of personal interest;
3. utilization of peer pressures as an impetus to student completion of instructional goals;
4. pupil practice in working cooperatively with others.

You can use group activity to build these four happy situations. The catch is that you can't use group activity to meet just any instructional objective. The objective determines whether or not group activity is an appropriate instructional method. Trying to meet an objective inappropriate to group activity through group activity, such as the application of arithmetic understandings to solve a simple equation, is what Dr. C. J. Jung criticized in his statement:

> When a hundred clever heads join in a group, one big nincompoop is the result because every individual is trummeled by the otherness of others.

On the other hand, some instructional activities are best performed through group activity. Examples of these activities include class governments, science demonstrations requiring two or more participants to manage the equipment, complex measurement activities requiring cooperative participation, dramatic activities, activities in social studies or civics involving data gathering from primary sources, and production-line simulations in industrial arts classes.

Five Steps to Successful Group Activity

Group activity is in itself a complex application by group members of a number of skills. In order to successfully manage group activity, "you have to teach them something first." The first step in directing group activity is teaching pupils what group activity is all about.

Through direct communication and teacher-pupil interaction you must build pupils' knowledge of the two essentials of group activity: (1) a common goal; and (2) cooperative work toward the goal. Direct communication and teacher-student interaction must lead pupils to understand that in a group work they must:

1. specifically define their group problem;
2. explore many ways to solve the problem;
3. choose one or more ways to solve the problem;
4. divide problem solving chores evenly among group members;
5. accept a peer as leader of the group.

As an ending exercise of this first step, it is a good idea to hold a "trial run" as a test of whether or not your pupils are ready to learn through group activity. Children should be taught that the trial run is a trial, that you will provide a small, easily managed problem for them to practice solving, and that you are simply setting the stage for pupils to later take a more active part in their own education. Remember, in using group activity as an instructional method, the instructional groups must know the process of group activity at the application level of learning.

The second step to effective group activity is to define the limits of group autonomy. These limits may be broad or narrow, but there must be limits. An elementary school teacher may be perfectly willing to allow several activity groups to choose their own method for learning about some topic from several alternatives that she provides. The teacher limits the group in providing the alternatives and in providing the topic. On the other hand, the teacher of a high school honors English class may be willing to allow an instructional group to choose any modern English novel as a subject for activity group study. The former teacher has planned a legitimate group activity while retaining a high degree of curricular control; the latter teacher has retained a minimum amount of control.

The amount of control retained depends upon the teacher's opinion of the learners' ability to make wise choices, and the teacher's opinion of what the local administration will stand for. Nevertheless, some limits, be they narrow or broad, must be planned, and these limits must be made clear to the students *before* they begin their group work. The surest way to destroy group activity is to limit group freedom after group activity has started.

The third step is the actual choice of the activity group members. Group size is dependent upon the nature of the activity. A group of two members makes sense for presenting a simple science demonstration, a group of thirty members may be needed for a mock class government situation. Small group discussion is maximumized by a group size of five to seven members.

Group member composition, as group size, is determined by the task. You don't want all of the shy children in one discussion group, nor do you want all of your natural leaders in one activity group. Simply explain this to prospective group members. Students will naturally want to form groups along friendship, neighborhood, or sex lines. However, once the pupils realize the need for certain people to avoid collecting in one group, they will accept this need and respect it. A large latitude of mutual choice of pupil group members will still be available, and pupils should be allowed this choice within the necessary limits set by you.

The fourth step is to allow the groups to choose their projects within the limits set by the first step. For the elementary teacher in the above example, this can be accomplished rather quickly, since the choices were severely limited. For the honors English teacher the group choice may occupy a great deal of time as group members digest critical reviews of various novels, and present their arguments to group members for choosing one or another novel. In the latter example this consultation of reviews and literary argument may so satisfy the teacher's goals that he may hope the group members never reach a decision.

In this discussion of project choice, it must be emphasized that group members must be upgrading familiarity and knowledge to the understanding and application levels of learning. Group activity used to build familiarity or knowledge of a subject results in the often criticized "pooling of ignorance." Avoid group activity for introductory pursuits.

The final step in teaching through group activity is teacher supervision of the functioning group or groups. This is the most difficult part of the process for the teacher. It is difficult because it is the teacher's job only to watch, to give moral support, to provide resource materials, but to avoid directly intervening. The groups will explore dead ends, will follow false trails, and will experience interpersonal conflicts among members. However, teacher intervention to alleviate these will destroy the effectiveness of appointed or elected group leaders, and will make impossible the development of a group *esprit de corps* which is essential to successful group activity. If you can't stand to allow pupils to flounder quite often as they grope their way through a problem, then avoid the instructional technique of group activity.

V. REVIEW THE FOUR METHODS

From this chapter you have learned about four teaching tools. These are the teaching methods of direct communication, teacher-student interaction, independent student activity, and group activity.

Much nonsense has been published about the goodness or badness of one method over another. None of the four methods is inherently effective, and none is inherently ineffective any more than a hammer or a screwdriver is inherently effective or ineffective. What makes the instructional method, or the hammer and screwdriver, effective is how it is used, and what it is used for. You would not expect much success from using a screwdriver in the task of driving a ten-penny nail into a two-by-four. Neither should you expect to be successful in raising pupils from the familiarity level of learning to the application level of learning through the exclusive use of direct communication.

The professional educator, be he classroom teacher or superintendent, is the educator with a full instructional methods tool kit, and the savy to know the right tool for the right job.

11

Use Interaction Analysis
to Improve Your Methods

What Interaction Does for You

Of the four methods of instruction described in the previous chapter, two methods are under the continuous direct control of the teacher. These are the methods of *direct communication* and *teacher-student discussion*. The extent to which either of these methods is used in the classroom is usually a matter of teacher guess, as is the fact of which method is being used at a particular time. Moreover, in pursuit of effective teacher-student discussion the teacher strives to maintain what the sociologists call *interaction* between teacher and students.

Interaction, the gut level involvement of both teacher and students in discussing a topic of importance to both, yields optimal learning results from the method of teacher-student discussion. Interaction between teacher and students is a delicate social process which is facilitated through respect by the teacher for students, and respect for the teacher by students. A condition of trust between teacher and students, and between student and student maximizes the possibility of classroom interaction. Each participant in interaction, including the teacher, must trust his fellows to avoid "stepping on his ego." It is just this type of trust that Mr. Kane worked to build in his adult education class. This is the type of trust that allowed Mrs. Lake to successfully guide Tony in his work with the number balance.

It should be evident that when words such as *respect, trust,* and *sincere human involvement* with others are used to describe a process, then the process must be a delicate one. It is.

Personal prejudices, rationalizations, the limited attention paying ability of students to teachers, the limited attention paying ability of teachers to students, and the unique ability of all humans to attend to personally selected aspects of their environments all mitigate against maintenance of the delicate process of interaction. Recognition of this fact is voiced each time an individual complains, "Whatever happened to the good conversations we used to have before T.V.?" The complaint really means, "Whatever happened to the successful human to human *interactions* we used to have before we grew too sophisticated to respect, trust, and be sincere with others?"

Analysis of the Trembling Tonsil

A powerful tool for helping professionals to improve their ability to get classroom interaction is now available. It is called *interaction analysis.* Interaction analysis is exactly what it says it is. Interaction analysis is an objective procedure for analyzing the teacher-student interaction for any classroom activity which involves a verbal exchange between teacher and students. The same procedure is equally usable for activities as diverse as show 'n tell in kindergarten, third-grade reading instruction, eighth-grade math, twelfth-grade history, or a principal-faculty in-service program.

The interaction analysis procedure described in this chapter was developed by Professor Ned Flanders of the Far West Laboratory for Educational Research and Development. Dr. Flanders' contribution of interaction analysis to education will, in future years, stand as important a "breakthrough" in education as was Galileo's contribution of the thermometer a "breakthrough" in physics. Flanders' procedure is a thermometer of interaction.

How You Can Use Interaction Analysis

Whether you are a primary teacher, intermediate teacher, high school teacher, principal, or central office executive, you can use interaction analysis to improve your ability to:

1. determine just what instructional method you have used during a given instructional session;
2. obtain a specific description of your instructional style;
3. get objective feedback as to teacher-student interaction patterns in your instructional sessions;
4. secure clues to how you can improve your approach to students to increase the probability of teacher-student interaction whenever you desire interaction;
5. talk about instruction with colleagues in specific terms;
6. think about your own instruction in a specific, disciplined manner.

Steps to Using Interaction Analysis

The first step in using interaction analysis is to get away from the too wide-spread and false notion that interaction analysis is a new technique for "snoopervisors" to use to bother you with another checklist. This is not so. The Flanders categorization system for describing interaction looks a little like a checklist, but it is totally divorced from the checklist concept. Interaction analysis is a system to help you improve your own instruction; it is not a teacher evaluation device.

The second step in using interaction analysis is to discard the false notion that what the Flanders categorization system calls "direct teacher influence" is bad, and what the system calls "indirect teacher influence" is good. This is not so. "Direct" and "indirect teacher influences" are types of teacher behavior which are practiced by all teachers in all situations. "Direct influence" is applicable to all instructional methods at some period in the use of each method, and "indirect influence" is applicable to the same methods at certain periods in the use of each method. Neither type of influence is intrinsically good or bad in itself. Direct and indirect teacher influence are simply defined terms within the Flanders categorization system.

Step three requires that you become familiar with the *Flanders Interaction Analysis Categorization System.* This system is reproduced in Figure 11-1.[1] Read it over. Develop a feel for the different

---

[1]Figure 11-1, "Categories for Interaction Analysis," is from Flanders, Ned A., *Interaction Analysis in the Classroom.* Ann Arbor, Michigan: The University of Michigan, School of Education, 1966. page 7.

TEACHER TALK	INDIRECT INFLUENCE	1.*	ACCEPTS FEELING: accepts and clarifies the feeling tone of the students in a non-threatening manner. Feelings may be positive or negative. Predicting or recalling feelings are included.
		2.*	PRAISES OR ENCOURAGES: praises or encourages student action or behavior. Jokes that release tension, not at the expense of another individual, nodding head or saying, "um hm?" or "go on" are included.
		3.*	ACCEPTS OR USES IDEAS OF STUDENT: clarifying, building, or developing ideas suggested by a student. As a teacher brings more of his own ideas into play, shift to category five.
		4.*	ASKS QUESTIONS: asking a question about content or procedure with the intent that a student answer.
	DIRECT INFLUENCE	5.*	LECTURING: giving facts or opinions about content or procedure; expressing his own ideas, asking rhetorical questions.
		6.*	GIVING DIRECTIONS: directions, commands, or orders to which a student is expected to comply.
		7.*	CRITICIZING OR JUSTIFYING AUTHORITY: statements intended to change student behavior from non-acceptable to acceptable pattern; bawling someone out; stating why the teacher is doing what he is doing; extreme self-reference.
STUDENT TALK		8.*	STUDENT TALK—RESPONSE: a student makes a predictable response to teacher. Teacher initiates the contact or solicits student statement and sets limits to what the student says.
		9.*	STUDENT TALK—INITIATION: talk by students which they initiate. Unpredictable statements in response to teacher. Shift from 8 to 9 as student introduces own ideas.
		10.*	SILENCE OR CONFUSION: pauses, short periods of silence and periods of confusion in which communication cannot be understood by the observer.

*There is NO scale implied by these numbers. Each number is classificatory, it designates a particular kind of communication event. To write these numbers down during observation is to enumerate, not to judge a position on a scale.

Figure 11-1. Categories for Interaction Analysis.

categories. Make a Xerox copy of Figure 11-1. You will need something more manageable than this book to use when doing a formal observation of the performance of a fellow teacher, or of *yourself*.

Notice that the system sorts all classroom verbal communication into ten categories, three of which define "direct teacher influence," four of which define "indirect teacher influence," two of which categorize "student talk" and one of which is reserved for describing classroom "silence or confusion." Do not yet criticize the system for oversimplifying the classroom situation. Remember, Flanders' interaction analysis is only designed to describe classroom verbal interaction, and is not designed to be all things to all men. The focus and the simplicity of Flanders' system is a strength, not a weakness.

Step four requires that you become familiar with the scoring system. Eventually, you will need to re-read this entire section to boost your familiarity with interaction analysis through knowledge and understanding to application. However, on this first reading settle for familiarity.

The scoring system is based upon a ten cell by ten cell matrix such as the one shown in Figure 11-2. Your matrix will need to be larger than the one in Figure 11-2 for reasons explained below.

The numbered cells (squares) in the matrix correspond to the numbered descriptions shown in Figure 11-1, the Flanders Interaction Analysis Categorization System. To complete step four you need to make a package of blank matrices like the sample shown in Figure 11-2.

Don't make a heat process ditto facsimile of Figure 11-2. It is too small. Line-out your matrix on a blank ditto master. Make each one of the one-hundred little squares (cells) measure ¾" across and ¾" down. There is nothing magical about those dimensions. They just fit most easily on a standard ditto master. Run off a few matrices to practice with as you read the rest of this chapter.

Step five involves actually using the interaction analysis system. You're ready to go.

To observe yourself you need a tape recording of about twenty minutes of a class session in which you are interested. Tape a class session in which you intend to get a teacher-student discussion

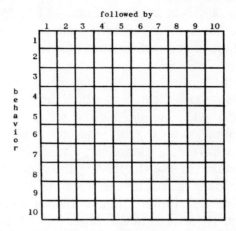

Figure 11-2. Matrix for Recording Classroom Behavior Tallies.

going, rather than a lecture or independent student activity. If you don't have a tape recorder, you need a pupil (high school) or colleague to sit in your classroom for ten or twenty minutes to chart your behavior. We have tried to train sixth-grade pupils to do the scoring job, but without success. The job seems to require a good deal of maturity, and some understanding of interaction.

Always begin marking the matrix in the block at the intersection of column ten, row ten (the 10-10 cell). This is a handy convention to get the ball rolling. Therefore, your first matrix mark looks like Figure 11-3.

Now you know that your next mark will go in one of the cells (squares) in row ten. This is because the rows indicate the last observed classroom behavior, and the columns (top numbers) indicate what *followed* the last observed behavior. For the sake of example, say the next behavior in the class is teacher lecture. The first tally was in the 10-10 cell (by convention), the next tally is placed in the box at row ten, column five (the 10-5 cell). This is shown in Figure 11-4.

You know that your next mark must go in one of the cells in row five. This is because a five (lecture) is the present behavior observed. What *follows* the lecture in three seconds will determine the column placement of the next tally.

Since few teacher lectures are completed in three seconds, assume that our example teacher continued to lecture for another

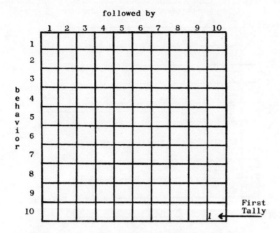

Figure 11-3. Beginning Matrix Marking.

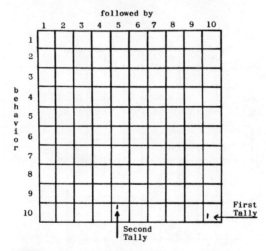

Figure 11-4. The First Observational Tally.

twenty-four seconds. This would require eight tallys in the row five, column five (the 5-5 cell) square indicating lecture followed by more lecture. This is illustrated in Figure 11-5.

Following the last lecture tally (5), the teacher then asked a short question. Since the question immediately followed a lecture sequence, remain in the five row, but mark a tally in the four column (the 5-4 cell) to indicate the change in teacher behavior. The proper placement is shown in Figure 11-6.

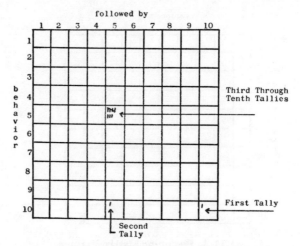

Figure 11-5. Adding the Lecture Tallies.

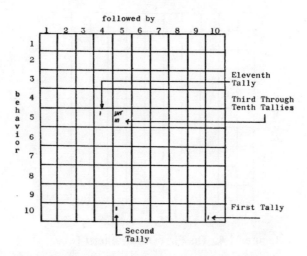

Figure 11-6. The Eleventh Tally-Teacher Question.

Then assume the three second question was followed by a student answer which continued for a total of nine seconds. Mark your own matrix, and then check with Figure 11-7 to compare.

Did you get it right? The first three seconds of student answer is represented by a tally in row four, column eight. It is placed in row four because it follows a teacher question (4 on the cate-

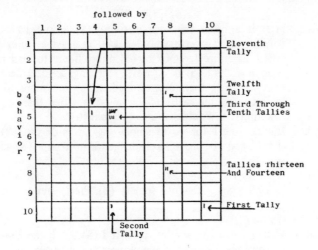

Figure 11-7. The Student Answer Tallies.

gorization system), and in column eight because the behavior *is* a student response to the teacher (8 on the categorization system).

Now you know why you need at least the suggested one-half square inch space in each block on your matrix. A twenty minute observation yields two-hundred tallies. The little blocks fill up fast.

Expect to fumble a little at first. Very soon you will find that you have memorized the ten categories of behavior, and you will no longer need to consult the categorization system sheet to find what the numbers mean. After all, on this first time through you already know that "5" means teacher lecture and "4" means teacher question.

Avoid using a watch to measure the three second period between each observation. Instead, develop a time sense by devices such as slowly tapping your pencil point three times on the matrix between tallies.

Now try a little practice. First, read the teacher-student script below. At the end of each three second segment, or change of category, find the number of the category from Figure 11-1 in parentheses. At the end of the script is a completed matrix for the segment. Test yourself by entering the behaviors on a blank matrix and then checking your matrix with the one following the script.

EXAMPLE ONE

Teacher: (10) It appears that pot smoking (5) is at least as habit forming as cigarette smoking (5), at least as injurious to health as cigarette smoking (5), more likely to lead to hard drug use than (5) is cigarette smoking, a good deal more expensive (5) than cigarette smoking, and more likely to lead to trouble with (5) legal authorities than cigarette smoking (5). Would you react to that (6)?

Pupil A: It's not legal for us to smoke cigarettes *or* pot (8). Why should grass be more likely to get us in trouble (8) with the law (8)?

Teacher: What do you think (2)?

Pupil A: I don't know. It's your society (8). Pretty hypocritical, I'd say (8).

Teacher: Go on (2).

Pupil A: Well, I mean (8), you're right. If I (8) break the law in the establishment's way by smoking (8) cigarettes, that's O.K. (8). But, if I break the law in my own way, with pot (8), man, they lock me up (8)!

Pupil B: He's right. They ought to legalize pot (9)!

From the short segment above you can tell something about the interaction that took place. Look at the most filled boxes in Figure 11-8. Five (lecture) and eight (pupil response) indicate a balance between teacher "telling behavior" and teacher-student interacting behavior. By looking at "what followed what" in Figure 11-8, you can see that the "eights" (student response) followed a "six" (teacher direction) once, and a "two" (teacher indirect encouragement) twice. "Ones," "twos," and "threes" are powerful means for getting pupils to interact with the teacher and with each other.

Most of the pupil comment in Example One was encouraged by the teacher in one way or another. However, the final student comment in the example was voluntarily offered without teacher encouragement, and constituted an indication that real interaction was beginning.

These are the types of clues to your instruction that you can get from interaction analysis. The same lesson could have been managed very differently as Example Two will show.

EXAMPLE TWO

Teacher: (10) It appears that pot smoking (5) is at least as habit forming as cigarette smoking (5). What do you say to that John (4)?

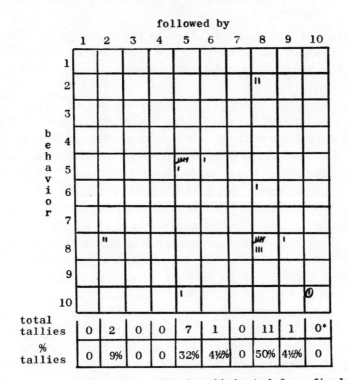

Figure 11-8. Matrix for Example One.

John: I suppose (8).
Teacher: Pot smoking is much more likely to lead to hard (5) drug use than is cigarette smoking (5).
Jim: I don't buy that. I know a guy who quit pot cold turkey (9).
Teacher·   The National Health Foundation pamphlet clearly states that pot (7) smoking is habit forming. Also, pot smoking (7) is much more expensive than cigarette smoking (5). Can you see that, Sue (4)?
Sue: No, I can't (8).
Teacher: Well, one marijuana cigarette costs as much as one and one-half (5) packs of regular cigarettes. Surely, that proves (5) that the marijuana habit is very expensive. Finally, (5) pot smoking is far more likely to lead to (5) trouble with the legal authorities (5) than cigarette smoking. I'm sure you all (5) see that while neither habit is (5) conducive to good

health, pot smoking (5) is far more harmful than cigarette smoking (5). Far more harmful (5).

Analysis of the Example Two matrix Figure 11-9 shows a preponderance of tallies in the 5-5 cell (lecture box). If the teacher was trying to get teacher-student interaction, he was not using a very powerful device for the purpose. Twice the teacher did use the question asking device (4) at the end of a lecture sequence, but the absence of time recorded in the 8-8 cell (student-talk box), or 9-9 cell indicates that the student responses were of three seconds or less duration. Three second responses concerning the type of material discussed in the example indicate a low level development of ideas by students. What happened to truncate the student responses is indicated by the row eight and row nine tallies (Figure 11-9). Twice student remarks were followed by additional teacher lecture, and once a student remark was followed by a teacher position justifying remark. The teacher should quickly see that to get interaction he needs to more frequently meet student remarks with a "one" (accepts feeling), a "two" (encouragement), or a "three" (uses student idea).

This does not mean that a teacher needs to always accept every student remark, no matter how inane, as a nugget of gold. It simply means that the way in which the teacher reacts to a student remark, in agreement or disagreement, has a great deal to do with both the likelihood of subsequent pupil response, and the quality of subsequent pupil response.

In summary, the patterns of responses on the matrices take on much meaning when examined on face.

Usually, for ten or twenty minute samples it is necessary to reduce the tallies to whole numbers on the matrices to simplify interpretation. This has been done in the following sample matrices which demonstrate common situations familiar to every professional. Each matrix depicts a ten-minute classroom interaction pattern. Sharpen your matrix interpretation skills by trying to guess what is going on. Be sure to refer to the category definitions in Figure 11-1 while working. The verbal descriptions of the samples follow the five sample matrices shown in Figures 11-10 to 11-14.

Sample one is easy. It describes a straight ten minutes of teacher lecture.

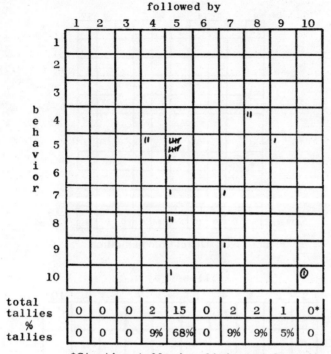

Figure 11-9. Matrix for Example Two.

The "tens" on the matrix in Figure 11-11 may have caused you some trouble. It helps to know whether they were silence or confusion. The clue to this is in an examination of the entire ten row. Examination of the ten row shows what followed the ten tallies. Tens followed by sevens (teacher criticism) usually means that the tens were confusion, since a teacher is unlikely to pause during a lecture, and then criticize pupils for keeping quiet during the pause. For the class described by sample two, if the teacher intent was a nice clean lecture, he was not successful since fifty percent of the time was spent in student confusion, teacher criticism of students, and teacher giving of directions. The Figure 11-11 matrix is in in reality a charting of the old, familiar lecture (5), pupil misbehavior (10), teacher bawls out class (7), teacher lays down law (6), teacher resumes lecture cycle prevalent in the

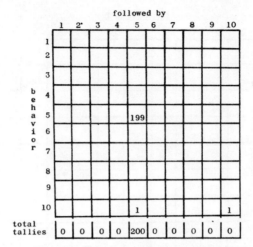

Figure 11-10. Direct Communication.

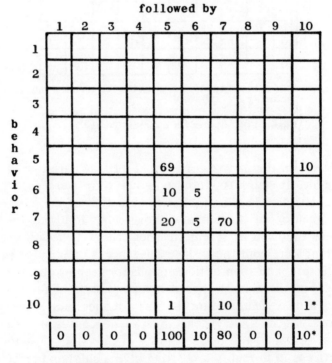

*Starting tally is eliminated from final scoring.

Figure 11-11. The Lecture-Misbehavior-Criticism-Rule Giving-Lecture Cycle.

classrooms of improperly trained, or inexperienced teachers. Interaction analysis can help these teachers recognize the merry-go-round they are on, and offer clues to help break the cycle.

Figure 11-12 plots a successful teacher-pupil discussion session. It shows that the teacher got, or kept the discussion ball rolling with only two direct questions (4), and encouraged the rest of the student talk with acceptance of student feeling (1), encouragement (2), or the use of student ideas (3). Note the many twos and threes followed by eights and nines (student talk). Student responses tended to be long (suggesting completeness and thought) as indicated by the numerous tallies in the 8-8 and 9-9 cells.

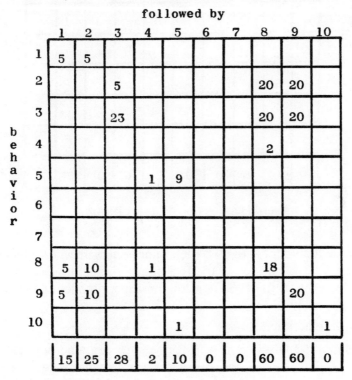

followed by

behavior	1	2	3	4	5	6	7	8	9	10
1	5	5								
2			5					20	20	
3			23					20	20	
4								2		
5				1	9					
6										
7										
8	5	10		1				18		
9	5	10							20	
10					1					1
	15	25	28	2	10	0	0	60	60	0

Figure 11-12. Teacher-Pupil Discussion.

Figure 11-13 shows a group student activity resulting from a short teacher direction (6) at the start of the period. After the teacher direction, subsequent activity consisted of student initiated talk (9). All this indicates is that the teacher did accomplish

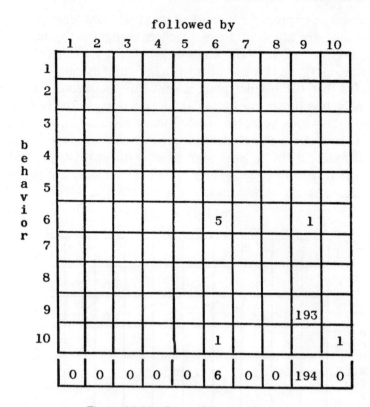

Figure 11-13. Group Student Activity.

independent student activity with a minimum of teacher direction.

Figure 11-14 is a plot of the ten minute period just prior to the scheduled visit to the classroom of the superintendent of schools.

Review Interaction Analysis

Interaction analysis is a way for you to examine how closely your intended instructional strategies match what is really going on in your classroom. To accomplish this end you need a copy of the Flanders Interaction Analysis Category System (Figure 11-1), and a few blank matrices (Figure 11-2). You also need a ten or twenty-minute tape recording of one of your instructional sessions, or a friend who is reasonably well practiced in translating your actions to the coded squares in the matrix.

That is all you need to gain objective descriptions of your

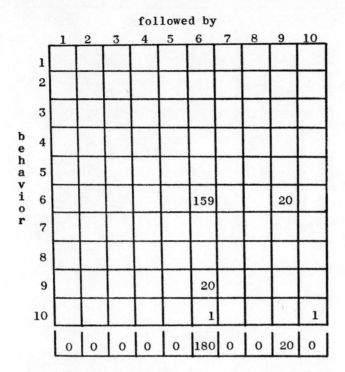

Figure 11-14. Preparation for a Visit by the Superintendent.

instruction. These descriptions have surprised many professionals, and have aided many professionals in improving their instruction. Instructional technique improvement has been particularly high in the method of teacher-student discussion.

You too will find that you get higher quality interaction in your discussions by "giving 'em a two."

12

Stimulate Your Students
Through Simulation

What Simulation Does for You

Simulation is an instructional technique that has only recently been applied to basic, general education. Conversely, simulation has long been used to accomplish the more specific goals of occupational training.

Professionals working toward general education goals can apply the powerful technique of simulation to enliven their classrooms, and to aid their pupils in developing deep understanding and permanent retention of subject matter to which simulation is applied.

This chapter will aid teachers in gaining an understanding of simulation, and will provide guidelines for utilizing the technique for both general and occupational education purposes.

Instructional Simulation Trains Salesmen

On the third floor of the Provident Mutual Insurance Company Headquarters are located a number of small cubicles. Each cubicle is furnished with a small table and two chairs. Periodically, each cubicle is occupied by a student insurance salesman and a company teacher acting as a "prospect." In these meetings students practice the selling techniques they have learned *via* direct communication from, and interaction with their teachers.

Early contacts between the fledgling salesman and his mock

prospect involve simple selling problems for the student. Initial contacts are planned so that the mock prospect represents himself as a person in need of insurance, a person very. near to awareness of the need, and a person inclined to ask only superficial and easy-to-answer questions concerning insurance plans. For the experienced salesman, the earliest mock selling sessions would be laughably easy. However, for the novices engaged in the procedure, the mock sessions provide challenge, excitement, involvement, and a non-threatening environment for testing recently learned techniques.

As the novice salesmen progress through the early, near automatic sales, instructors prescribe tougher assignments. Mock prospects present ever more complex situations where the need for insurance is not so evident as before. Also, the mock prospect asks progressively more complex questions pressing the novice's knowledge of the company in particular, and insurance in general.

Upon completion of the carefully planned entry program, the young insurance salesman approaches his first real prospect with considerable experience in the soul to soul confrontation that selling is. He achieved this experience through a carefully planned curriculum partially activated by the technique of mock selling, a sales simulation.

Instructional Simulation Trains Airplane Pilots

In an air conditioned flight line shack at the Hawthorne School of Aeronautics in Georgia are contained a row of box-like objects. Within each of the boxes is an authentic set of aircraft controls and instruments arranged exactly as in an aircraft cockpit. The machines are third generation descendants of the venerable Link Trainer. Anyone strapped inside of one of the boxes, shut off from the world, soon forgets he is in a box. His every sense and nerve tells him that he is part of an aircraft in flight. Some pilots have been known to try to "bail out" when their simulator control panels told them of a hopeless condition.

The first time that the trusting student is strapped into his instrument trainer box, everything possible is done to arrange the environment to help him succeed. Altitude controls are locked to assure the student will hold a constant altitude that is the envy of a veteran airline captain. Roll and yaw controls are managed by the instructor to allow the student practically no margin for error. The simulator controls are set so that the student experiences glassy smooth, windless flying conditions so ideal as to be impossible under actual flying circumstances. Engine and power transmission instruments present a picture of a perfectly functioning aircraft.

Under the reassuring guidance of his teacher, the student pilot learns from his initial simulator flights that he can control an airplane through reference to a set of remarkably accurate round dials and figures on his control panel.

Very soon the student pilot also learns that simulators, once locked for unrealistically ideal conditions, can be unlocked for ever more realistic and treacherous conditions. The instructor insures that the student in the box will almost always succeed in completing his simulated flight, but as the student gains skill in instrument flying, the simulated flying task will become increasingly more difficult.

Systems Analysts Use Simulation

The RAND Corporation in Santa Monica, California, has refined the teaching technique of simulation to a high art. RAND analysts have shown a willingness to analyze the operation of any human endeavor, and to devise simulation techniques to train present and prospective workers in the tasks required. RAND, as much as any other company in the analysis-teaching field, has recognized simulation as a powerful tool for systems analysis, for research, and for teaching.

Avoid Confusion of Simulation Uses

Systems analysis, research, and teaching are the three tasks for which the technique of simulation is suited. That simulation is used for three related, but different, tasks is what makes reading the education literature on simulation confusing. Avoid confusion. Understand that this chapter is describing simulation as a teaching technique. Simulation can be a powerful technique to aid systems analysis and research, but you won't learn anything about those uses here. Simulation is described in this chapter only as it applies to what you do—to instruction.

The instructional technique of simulation is not listed in the U.S. Department of Health, Education and Welfare publication, *Standard Terminology for Instruction in State and Local School Systems.* Moreover, simulation was not listed as one of the four instructional methods described in Chapter 10 of this book. Simulation is treated here as an instructional technique deriving either from the method of *independent student activity,* or from the method of *group activity.* From which method simulation emerges depends upon whether the simulations are designed for a single student, or for a group of students. Realize that everything that was said in Chapter 10 about independent student activity and group activity applies to simulation.

The examples of simulation use that you have read concerning simulation as a training device for insurance salesmen and aircraft pilots are obvious uses of simulation to build skills at the *application* level of learning. In fact, simulation was used as an example technique to illustrate the "Teacher Action to Build Level; Motor Skills" in Table I on page 20 of this book. Alert instructors have always made use of simulation whenever they have worked both to build learner skills to the application level of learning, and can buy, build, or arrange classroom conditions to simulate the real-life situation for which learners are being prepared. In most secondary schools we find: driver training instructors making use of auto simulators, or specially prepared real autos; home economics teachers using shiny ovens and sewing machines in simulated home settings; industrial arts teachers who have recently abandoned student doorstop making in favor of simulated classroom production lines; dramatics teachers leading pupils to produce superbly complex school productions; journalism teachers guiding students in the publication of periodic newspapers and school magazines; and physics instructors with their layman-perplexing labs in which pupils simulate the discovery of physical science principles under the guidance of ubiquitous PSSC materials. All of these professionals are using the technique of simulation.

How You Can Use Simulation in Your Classroom

Uses of simulation to prepare students for applying their understanding and knowledge of the practical arts are often obvious. A less obvious use of simulation is to use the technique for helping learners achieve the *understanding* level of learning in a field outside of the practical arts. An example will illustrate.

Charles Peck is a sixth-grade teacher in the Ardsley Public Schools. He adapted the simulation technique to exercises designed to aid pupils in gaining an understanding of basic economics principles. Mr. Peck directed his simulations as part of a year-long social studies program. The first of a series of his economic simulations is reported below.

Mr. Peck organized his social studies class of twenty-six children into six work groups. The groups were arranged as follows:

Group A—six children
Group B—six children
Group 1—four children
Group 2—four children
Group 3—four children
Group X—two children

Group X was not part of the simulation. The children in this group served as "teacher helpers."

Groups A and B were provided with equal, but small amounts of paper plus scissors, twelve-inch rulers, and crayons. Groups 1, 2, and three were provided with a supply of play money, and a large amount of paper.

The children were carefully prepared to participate in the simulation. Through direct instruction and teacher-pupil inter-action, students were taught that the simulation was to be a social studies lesson with a serious purpose. Children learned that Groups A and B represented large industrial nations such as the U.S. or U.S.S.R. They learned that Groups 1, 2, and 3 represented small, non-industrial nations such as Pakistan or Cuba. The children understood that each of the five groups was to compete with the others in trying to fill "assignments" listed on the blackboard by Mr. Peck. Mr. Peck listed the assignments which told the children to deliver to Group X:

Groups A and B   Fifty dollars in play money.
Group 1   A six-inch, black crayon line or white paper.

| Group 2 | A blue paper triangle three inches on each side. |
| Group 3 | A green paper rectangle five inches by two inches. |

The correctness of color and dimensions was checked compulsively by the children in Group X, leaving Mr. Peck free to change assignments, and to observe the activity.

Mr. Peck arranged the initial distribution of materials so that no one group had all of the materials necessary to complete the assignment. He also taught the pupils that it would be necessary for them to trade between groups in order to complete any of the assignments. Mr. Peck designated a table in the cénter of the classroom as the only place where "negotiations" for trades, or actual trades of materials could take place. He restricted the children so as to allow only one group member to be absent from each group table at any one time. He cautioned the children that stiff "fines" of play money and materials would be levied for violations of the table leaving rule.

Mr. Peck set the children to work with the simulation. The children quickly realized that, as Mr. Peck said, they could not complete their assignments without obtaining additional materials, and trades between groups began to take place.

The children in the two groups provided with a "manufacturing capability" (scissors, crayons, and rulers) soon learned to maintain their advantage by not trading manufacturing tools for "raw materials" (paper). One of the numbered groups was able to trade paper and play money for a crayon and twelve-inch rule, but this did not happen again. Instead, the lettered groups traded finished products needed by the small groups for ever increasing supplies of play money and paper.

Mr. Peck had previously told the children that the object of the exercise was to fill the largest number of teacher requests for finished products in the allotted thirty minutes of the exercise. As soon as a group filled its request, Mr. Peck changed the group's assignment to one of the other assignments shown on page 177.

Predictably, the larger groups, initially supplied with crayons, rulers, and scissors, far outpointed the smaller groups.

After the simulation exercise was completed, Mr. Peck held a teacher-student discussion of the activity. Children readily drew analogies between the game experience, and the difficulties faced by non-industrial nations in the modern world. In discussion children asked: "Why don't nations without machines 'go broke' like we did?" "Why don't we be fair and give them some machines?" "What did the paper mean?" "Who writes the stuff on the board so the nations know what to make?"

The questions and the teacher-pupil discussions they encouraged indicated that Mr. Peck had moved children to a knowledge and rudimentary understanding of a few basic economic truths concerning relationships among modern nations. Additional simulations, of increasing sophistication, helped Mr. Peck to build in his pupils a greater understanding of how international relations operate. Specific descriptions of four of these simulations can be found in *Grade Teacher* magazine.[1]

The Mr. Peck example is a definition of what we mean by simulation as a teaching technique. The technique is one tool for instruction, and can never carry the whole of any curriculum plan, or even one set of working objectives within a curriculum plan. However, simulation is an extremely powerful instructional tool which cannot be ignored by any modern professional.

Six Basic Principles to Guide You in Implementing Simulation

Six basic principles are essential for successful simulation and management. These are:

1. Simulation is a special case of independent student activity, or of group student activity. Use the simulation technique to build upon existing familiarity and knowledge to reach understanding or application; pre-sell pupils to accept the goal of the activity; pre-teach children to manage the activity themselves; and once the simulation is started, leave the children alone to succeed or fail on their own efforts.
2. Teachers who use simulation must do more than simply teach children to "play the game." The teacher must see to it that pupils make the transfer from simulation to the real world activity or process under study.

---

[1] Charles Christine and Dorothy Christine. "Four Simulation Games That Teach," *Grade Teacher*. Vol. 85, No. 2. October, 1967. pp. 109-120.

3. Simulations are not foolproof. They can and do occasionally fail either in execution or transfer. The failure of a simulation, especially in execution, can be almost as valuable a learning experience as a successful run.
4. In order to invent successful simulations teachers must:
   a. fully understand the process or concept they wish to teach
   b. define clear working objectives
   c. invest hard work in preparing scenarios
   d. write-out detailed self-instructions specifying materials needed, furniture arrangements, and sequences of events
5. Simulations are noisy. Children, especially young children, become involved, excited, and vocal during simulations. Noise can (and should) be controlled, but it will never be absent.
6. Simulations must be planned in series. Begin with very simple, easy to manage exercises which practically guarantee student success both in the simulation and in transfer of training from simulated situation to reality. Gradually complicate the simulations to finally match whatever level of complexity is required by your objectives. Recognize that student success in simulation is not measured by the goodness of student performance, but by the complexity of the task he can manage.

The insurance salesman and student pilot examples of simulation activities were designed to provide an overview of the easy-to-real structuring which is essential to successful simulation. The Mr. Peck example was a microscopic view of the initial segment of a series of simulation activities designed to carry part of the teaching load of a year-long Modern World social studies unit.

It is a time consuming and difficult process for the classroom teacher to devise and plan his own simulations, but it is not impossible. Mr. Peck used a little imagination, a few simple materials, and a great deal of planning effort to produce his instructional tool.

There are a great many ready-made simulation scenarios on the commercial market today. Professionals interested in making use of the simulation technique should investigate the commercial programs available before devoting great amounts of time and effort to producing their own. The major sources of commercial simulations are:

1. Abt Associates., 55 Wheeler Street, Cambridge, Massachusetts 02136. Abt has a wide selection of simulations for many subjects, and grade levels from upper elementary through college. Write for their listing.

2. Boocock, S. S. and E. O. Schild. *Simulations Games in Learning.* Sage Publications Inc., California. This book contains instructions for simulations appropriate to junior and senior high school social situations, U.S. History, and Problems of Democracy.

3 Education Development Center, 15 Mifflin Place, Cambridge, Massachusetts 02138. *Man—A Course of Study.* Complete one year fifth grade social studies unit which includes simulations.

4. Garrison, William A. *Simsoc, A Manual for Participants.* Ann Arbor, Michigan: Campus Publishers; 1966. These simulations cross subject lines to combine economics, general history, geography, sociology, and citizenship. Suitable for high school. Requires groups of 20 to 60 pupils and four separate rooms.

5. Gearon, John D. "Labor vs. Management: A Simulation Game." *Social Education.* 30:421. October, 1966. This simulation, usable in either junior or senior high schools, touches sociology, history, economics, and problems of democracy.

6. Gearon, John D. "War or Peace: A Simulation Game." *Social Education.* 30:521. November, 1966. This simulation is suitable for either junior or senior high school, and is suitable for general history instruction.

7. Helburn, Nicholas. *The American High School Geography Project* Dr. Nicholas Helburn, Association of American Geographers, Boulder, Colorado. An eleven unit simulation (available separately). Each unit takes about three weeks to complete. Units are used for developing basic geography concepts.

8. Interact, P.O. Box 202, Lakeside, California 92040. Simulations for many subjects and grade levels. Write for their listing. This company is the source for the much discussed

Disunia, a pre-civil war, U.S. History simulation for junior high school and up.

9. Portola Institute, 1115 Merrill St., Menlo Park, California 94025. This company lists a selection of social studies simulations for all grades.

10. Scott Foresman and Company, 1900 E. Lake Ave., Glenview, Illinois 60025. *Dangerous Parallel,* a high school history simulation.

11. Simulations Inc., 2147 University Ave., St. Paul, Minnesota 55114. This company lists social studies simulations for junior high school and high school.

12. Western Publishing Company, School and Library Dept., 850 Third Avenue, New York, New York 10022. This company lists many simulations for junior high school and high school social studies. This is the source for the guidance game, *Generation Gap.*

Review Simulation

It was shown in this chapter that many high school teachers, particularly in the occupational training field, have used simulation techniques for a long time. The chapter indicated that simulation can also be used for work toward academic learning goals, particularly in the social studies.

One example set of instructions for an elementary school social studies simulation was presented to illustrate the simulation concept, and also to demonstrate that the technique can be adapted to elementary school instruction.

Six basic principles for guiding simulations were detailed: (1) teach the game; (2) teach for transfer; (3) failure recovery; (4) use care in design; (5) expect noise; and (6) manage complexity.

Teachers were encouraged to plan their own simulations, but cautioned that simulation planning takes much time. It was pointed out that the benefits of simulation can be enjoyed through purchase of one of the many published simulation scenarios.

13

Practical Pointers
on Programmed Instruction

Rodney Rat Illustrates
The First Operational Step

Once upon a time there was a very small, very bright laboratory rat who lived at the State University of Iowa. His name was Rodney. Every day Rodney waited patiently for his psychologist to bring him food pellets precisely at four o'clock each afternoon.

One afternoon Rodney was alarmed when his psychologist failed to bring his four o'clock dinner. Rodney waited and fretted for twenty-four hours, and still his psychologist brought him no food. Rodney was very hungry.

Finally, Rodney watched with disappointment as his psychologist arrived twenty-four hours late not with food, but with a long, shiny tube which he inserted in Rodney's cage.

Rodney examined the bottom of the tube. He found a small cup which smelled like food, but contained none. He twisted his head to look up at the trap door leading from cup to tube. That too smelled like food, but there was no food to be found. While looking up at the trap door, Rodney's pink eye fell on a small lever sticking out from the trap door. Rodney straightened his head, stood on his hind feet, and braced himself on the lever for a closer smell of the odd protuberance. As he placed his front paws on the lever, the lever descended with a loud "click." Rodney's paws crashed to the ground with Rodney close behind. On reaching the ground Rodney found a round food pellet in the cup at the bottom of the tube.

Rodney ate his pellet with relish, and returned to the lever. Again there was a loud "click," and again Rodney heard a food pellet drop into his cup.

Many clicks later, Rodney happily returned to his bed at the corner of his cage. As he prepared to take a short nap before returning to the tube, one of Rodney's friends from a neighboring cage asked, "What's all of the 'clicking' going on over there?"

Rodney replied sleepily, "I've just trained my psychologist to give me a food pellet every time he hears that lever click."

Motivation Is the Key to Programing

The parable of Rodney the rat illustrates the first operational step in programmed learning. The first operational step is to get the learner to make a response to the program *hardware*. If this response is rewarded, food was a powerful reward for hungry Rodney, then it is likely the learner will make future responses to the hardware. Thus, the key to successful program learning is to first motivate the learner to respond to the *hardware* that carries the program. It is necessary to clarify what is meant by *hardware*, and what is meant by *program*.

How You Can Tell Hardware from Program

The "teaching machines" which were supposed to revolutionize instruction by the early 1970's are part of the *hardware* of programmed instruction. Teaching machine hardware is available as little boxes which look like adding machines advancing rolls of paper one click at a time. Other teaching machines appear as tiny slide projectors designed to advance rolls of film one click at a time. Some teaching machines consist of round sheets of paper which fit, record-like, on a platform covered by a lid which exposes only a small portion of the paper disc, and contain a lever which changes the exposed part of the disc one click at a time. The hardware of the most expensive teaching machines is a typewriter electrically connected to a program director either as simple as the mechanism on a mechanical music box, or as complex as an electronic computer. Whether music box or computer, the function of the hardware is to move the instructional program forward one click at a time. Some teaching machine "hardware" is simply a book which looks suspiciously like an ordinary workbook, but which leads the student through its content one click at a time.

The material being moved one click at a time is the *program*. It is the goodness of the program that determines the value of the teaching machine, be it electronic computer or workbook. In programmed learning *what* is being advanced one click at a time is more important than the machinery doing the clicking. If hungry Rodney had received a steel pellet, rather than a food pellet, from his pellet dispenser he would have quickly lost interest in the device. Your pupils will demand a much higher quality nourishment than Rodney.

Try On Linear Programing for Size

Everybody talks about programmed learning, but few teachers do anything about it. Let's do something about it. Try this. For the next few pages fold a piece of paper so as to cover the print in this book, but leave the outside (away from the binding) margin clear so you can see the horizontal line extending beyond the print margin to the edge of the page. This book, and your piece of paper are your programmed learning *hardware*. Follow the instructions below to advance through this program about programmed learning. First, place your paper *under* the line going horizontally across the page below, and follow the instruction above the line. Go!

_____ Move Your Paper Down To The Next Line.   **A.**

1. Whenever you see a little line like this _____ it

    means you are to write a response. On a blank line

    you are to write a _____. (fill-in blank)
                            (1)

    Fill-in blank (1) and move your paper to line "C".

                                                              B.

                                              1. response

2. One type of program works in this way. You get a little

    bit of information, and then write a _____ to
                                              (2)
    it.

    Fill-in blank and move your paper to line "D".

                                                              C.

186 PRACTICAL POINTERS ON PROGRAMMED INSTRUCTION

2. response

3-4. The writing of responses to the program keeps you
alert to, and involved with the program. Therefore,
you are required to write responses so you will be

_____ and _____.
        (3)   (4)

Move to line "E".

D. _____

3. alert 4. involved

5-7. You write _____ so you will be _____
                (5)   (6)
to, and _____with the programmed
             (7)
material.

Move to line "F".

E. _____

5. responses 6. alert 7. involved

8. This type of program contains a great deal of repetition
of material. Learning material is repeated to aid
learning. One learning aid contained in this type of
program is _____.
                      (8)
Move to line "G".

F. _____

8. repetition

9-11. Student motivation in this type of program is sus-
tained by having the student write a _____
                                          (9)

to keep him _____ and _____.
                 (10)   (11)

Move to line "H".

_____ G.

9. response   10. alert   11. involved

12.   Student learning from the program is aided by much

         _____of material.
                (12)

         Move to line "I".

_____ H.

                                     12. repetition

13.   While student learning from this type of program is

         aided by repetition, it is also aided by the student's

         feeling of satis.action from giving the correct response.

         Giving the correct response gives the student a feeling

         of _____.
                 (13)

         Move to line "J".

_____ I.

                                     13. satisfaction

14-16.   To review, writing a _____ keeps the
                                  (14)

         student _____ to, and _____
                     (15)   (16)

         in the program.

         Move to line "K".

_____ J.

                14. response   15. alert   16. involved

17.   Almost always responding with the correct response helps

         student motivation by giving the student _____.
                                                        (17)

         Move to line "L".

_____ K.

                                     17. satisfaction

18.   Student learning is insured by _____
                                               (18)

         of program material.

         Move to line "M".

_____ L.

                                     18. repetition

19-20. This type of program is called a <u>linear</u> <u>program</u>.
It expands the student's knowledge in tiny steps.
A program expanding student knowledge in tiny steps
is called a _____ _____.
                (19)   (20)
Move to line "N".

M.
_____
19. linear 20. program

21-22. A linear program expands the student's knowledge in

_____ _____.
    (21)   (22)
Move to line "O".

N.
_____
21. tiny 22. steps

23. In order to learn from a linear program the student must
write a _____ in each blank.
            (23)

O.
_____
23. response

24-26. The writing of a _____ is designed to
               (24)
keep a student _____ to, and _____
           (25)   (26)
in the linear program.

P.
_____
24. response 25. alert 26. involved

27. The linear program is designed so that the student is
likely to make only correct responses. This gives the
student a feeling of _____.
                  (27)

Q.
_____
27. satisfaction

28-29. The likelihood of correct student response is insured by advancing the linear program in tiny

_____ and in providing much _____
     (28)   (29)

of program material.

R.
_____

28. steps 29. repetition

30-31. To review, a _____ program requires that
                    (30)

the student write a _____ in each blank.
                    (31)

                                                        S.
_____

                    30. linear 31. response

32-33. The actual writing of responses by the student helps

keep the student _____ to, and _____
                        (32)   (33)

in his work.

                                                        T.
_____

                    32. alert 33. involved

34. Student responses to linear program items must always

be correct to give the student _____ .
                                      (34)

                                                        U.
_____

                    34. satisfaction

35-36. Correctness of student responses is maximized by the

presentation of linear program material in tiny

_____ , and by a great deal of _____
     (35)   (36)

of program material.

                                                        V.
_____

                    35. steps 36. repetition
                    END PROGRAM
_____

Review Linear Programing

You have learned what a linear program is by using a simple
teaching machine containing the required program. The same
material could have been presented on a mechanical gadget that
would have saved you the bother of fumbling with paper and
book, or on some type of on-line computer presentation. However, the crucial aspect of the learning exercise was not the
mechanics of presentation, but was the goodness of the material
that made-up the program.

If you learned that the linear programing technique requires
repetitious, correct written responses to maximize learner alertness, involvement, and satisfaction in written material that
advances learner knowledge in tiny steps, then our program was a
success.

The linear programing technique is well suited to simple tasks such as demonstrated above. We used linear programing to familiarize you with the linear programing technique, and to build your knowledge and understanding of the process. To boost your understanding to the application level of learning you need to practice writing a program for your own pupils according to linear programing principles. Keep your initial program goals as uncomplicated as we kept ours in the example above, and you will have little trouble.

Where Working Objectives Aid Program Writing

By "initial program goals" we mean a statement of exactly what you intend your program to accomplish. This statement should be in the "working objectives" form described in Chapter 4.

For example, when we wrote our program on linear programing we used the following working objectives:

SUBJECT: Linear Programing

A. Reader will be familiar with the purpose of *the response* in programmed learning.

B. Reader will know:
  1. the programing definition of *response*
  2. the constituents of linear programing
     a. small steps   d. satisfaction
     b. involvement   e. repetition
     c. alertness

C. Reader will understand the function of:
  1. written responses   4. student satisfaction
  2. student involvement   5. repetition
  3. student alertness   6. small steps

The sample program required that you write thirty-six responses to program items contained in twenty-one program *frames.* A *frame* is one complete segment of a program, and was inclosed by the lettered lines in the sample program above.

When to Use Linear Programing
in Your Classroom

In your own classroom you may find uses for linear programs in aiding you to define terms for students, aid students in their grasp of a simple arithmetic or mathematical process, help students grasp a theoretical scientific principle, or aid students to develop a knowledge of a single writing convention such as comma placement. Some writers support linear programing as a vehicle for carrying the entire load of arithmetic, English grammar, or spelling instruction. We do not. We present the linear programing technique as one teaching tool to be used when professional judgement indicates that a particular learner and learning task are suited to linear program presentation.

Try on Intrinsic Branching Programing

A programing technique that will carry a heavier teaching load than linear programing was devised by Norman Crowder of U. S. Industries. Crowder devised the *Intrinsic Branching Method* of program writing.

A sample of the branching technique has been provided below. The sample is not represented as a complete program. The Intrinsic Branching Method is quite complex, and requires a book-length program for most concepts. Work through the branching program below, not to learn anything about exponent usage or astromony, but simply to acquire a feel for the Intrinsic Branching Method of programing. Use the same paper moving technique with this program that you used with the linear programing example.

F
R
A
M
E

1

Any discussion of astronomy involves the use of measurements of great distances. The nautical mile (1 mile = 6000 feet) is a possible measurement unit in discussion of the solar system, but for distances beyond the solar system the unit of measure must be expanded to the:

  1. light year (go to frame 3).

  2. sidereal day (go to frame 2)

F
R
A
M
E

2

You came from frame 1.

Your answer, sidereal day, is incorrect.

The unit of measure for distances beyond the solar system is the light year. Sidereal day is a measure of time.

Now return to frame 1.

You came from frame 1.

Your answer, light year, is correct.

F

R   The light year is used for measuring distances so great

A   as to be incomprehensible by any normal experience. The dis-

M   tance, in miles, of one light year is calculated by multiplying

E   the speed of light (186,000 miles per second), times the number

       of seconds in a minute (60), times the number of minutes in an

       hour (60), times the number of hours in a day (24), times the

3   average number of days in one year (365). The multiplication

       of the five factors yields a distance of 5,865,696,000,000

       miles which is the light year equivalent in miles.

       For discussions such as this it is convenient to round

the figure and say that a light year is equal to six trillion

miles. It is even more convenient to use an "exponent short-

hand" and express the 6,000,000,000,000 figure as:

    1. 6×10^{12} (go to frame 5)

    2. 6×10^{13} (go to frame 4)

You came from frame 3.

Your answer, 6×10^{13}, is incorrect.

F

R   To express a numeral as an exponent simply count the zeros

       in the raw numeral, and insert that numeral as the exponent. F

A   example, $100 = 1 \times 10^{2}$ (two zeros in 100; therefore, an exponent

M   of 2 is attached to the numeral 10. Then $5000 = 5 \times 10^{3}$. Using

E   this zero counting trick we find that six trillion is equal to

       $6 \div 1,000,000,000,000$. With twelve zeros in one trillion, the

4   proper exponent for increasing one ten to one trillion is 12;

       therefore, six trillion is equal to 6×10^{12}.

       Check yourself. Put the rounded distance from the Earth

to the Sun in exponent form. The distance is 93,000,000 miles.

    1. 93×10^{8} (go to frame 7)

    2. 93×10^{6} (go to frame 6)

    3. 93×10^{5} (go to frame 9)

You came from frame 3.

Your answer, $6. \times 10^{12}$, is correct

FRAME 5

The nearest star to the Earth is at a distance of approximately 253×10^{12} miles, or 4.3 light years. This nearest star is called Alpha Centauri. Interestingly, the nearest star to the Earth is not the brightest star when viewed from Earth. The star which appears brightest to an observer during an Earth night is Sirius, which is estimated as being 8.8 light years from Earth.

Astronomers consider Alpha Centauri and Sirius as our neighbors since they are a part of our:

1. planetary system (go to frame 12)

2. solar system   (go to frame 11)

3. galaxy   (go to frame 10)

You came from frame 4.

Your answer, 93×10^6 is correct.

FRAME 6

That's right. You counted only the zeros, separated the millions designator, and used the number of zeros as the exponent for ten. Now try putting the rounded light year figure of 6,000,000,000,000 miles into exponent form.

1. 6×10^{12} (go to frame 5)

2. 6×10^{13} (go to frame 8)

Jan. 21
Jan. 23
Jan. 28
Feb. 4
Feb. 8
Feb. 21
Feb. 23
Feb. 28
Mar. 3
Mar. 5
Mar. 7
Mar. 8
Mar. 20
Mar. 22
Mar. 24
Mar. 27
Mar. 28
Mar. 29
Mar. 30
Apr. 3
Apr. 4

You came from frame 4.

Your answer, 93×10^8, is incorrect.

FRAME 7

No, you counted <u>all</u> of the figures in 93,000,000, and not just the zeros. You count only the zeros to determine your exponent. Go back and read frame 4 again carefully.

FRAME 8

You came from frame 6.

Your answer, 6×10^{13}, is incorrect.

No, you counted <u>all</u> of the figures in 6,000,000,000,000, and not just the zeros. You count only the **zeros** to determine your exponent. Go back and read frame 4 again carefully.

FRAME 9

You came from frame 4.

Your answer, 93×10^5, is incorrect.

You must have counted all of the zeros except one. You probably did this since there is already one zero in the ten to which the exponent is attached. Do not do this. Count <u>all</u> of the zeros, and express the total number of zeros that you count as the exponent attached to the ten. Return to frame 4, and try again.

FRAME 10

You came from frame 5.

Your answer, galaxy, is correct.

Stop here. You have completed the program.

FRAME 11

You came from frame 5.

Your answer, solar system, is incorrect.

The solar system consists of the star we call the Sun, and the nine planets that surround the Sun.

The next larger astronomical unit from the solar system is the <u>galaxy</u>. While there is only one sun in our solar system, our Sun is one of a grouping of stars in our galaxy, which is called the Milky Way. Our Sun, Alpha Centauri, and Sirus are three of 1×10^9 stars estimated to be in our galaxy. Now return to frame 5.

F
R
A
M
E

12

You came from frame 5.

Your answer, planetary system, is incorrect.

The geography of astronomy usually makes two major groupings or classifications of heavenly bodies. The smallest classification of heavenly bodies is the <u>solar system</u>. Only one solar system is known; that containing our Sun and its' nine planets. However, one astronomer has speculated that several trillion solar systems exist.

A solar system is defined by a star (or stars) and the planets revolving about the star.

The next larger classification is the <u>galaxy</u>. The galaxy is an identifiable grouping of stars. Our galaxy, the Milky Way, contains as estimated one hundred billion stars.

Now go to frame 11.

Review Intrinsic Branching Programing

Notice that the Branching Method involved a linear aspect in that a student who had a knowledge of the material could move quickly through the twelve frame program in four jumps as shown in Figure 13-1. Essentially, this is the same as the linear program, except that the repetition aspect of linear programing was eliminated. The student able to progress very rapidly, with minimum repetition, can do so in a branched program.

The student unfamiliar with the "light year" term was "branched" to frame 2 for a brush-up on the discrimination between light year and sidereal day, and then returned to the main program at frame 1. More development of the light year concept, and some repetition steps could, and should be added to the light year branch.

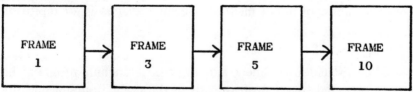

Figure 13-1. Main Branch of Astronomy Program Example.

The student unfamiliar with exponents was given some rule-of-thumb assistance from branches out of frame 3. Frame 4 provided a count-the-zeros rule for reducing large figures to exponents. For the student unfamiliar with the solar system—galaxy terminology repetition step at frame 6, and then a movement back to the main program at frame 5.

The student branched from frame 6 to frame 8 was assumed to have made a lucky guess of the answer to frame 6. Frame 8 is a "catch frame" inserted as a guard against guessers.

Frame 4 also provided two "diagnostic branches" to correct the two most common errors made by students in applying the count-the-zeros exponent rule. Frame 7 was designed to correct the student who counted *all* of the numerals to derive the exponent. Frame 9 was designed to correct the student who subtracted a zero to allow for the zero in the ten to which the exponent is attached.

From frame 5 there are two "teaching branches" to aid both the student unfamiliar with the solar system-galaxy terminology (to frame 12), and the student slightly familiar with the terminology (to frame 11). Both branches lead back to frame 5, and on to the end of the sample program at frame 10 The progression of Intrinsic Branching in the sample astronomy program is shown in diagram form in Figure 13-2.

The Intrinsic Branching Method of programing is a good deal more sophisticated than the linear method. The Branching Method is also more adapted to the individual student's learning pace than is the linear method. If teaching frames (such as frames 2 and 4), diagnostic frames (such as frames 7 and 9), repetition frames (such as frame 6), and catch frames (such as frame 8) are incorporated in the program, then the program becomes a tutor. The mechanical tutor is no better than the effort and ingenuity that the program writer builds into the program, but no worse than the live teacher who roars along the main branch of content development without consideration of supplementary teaching, diagnosis, or repitition.

Guidelines to Program Selection

This discussion of linear and intrinsic branching programs has been prepared to aid professionals in the evaluation and selection of programs now in existence, or soon to appear. Three guidelin s

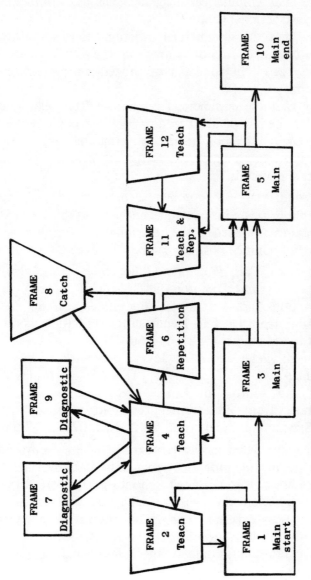

Figure 13.2. Flow Diagram of Astronomy Program Example.

should be applied to the evaluation of programmed learning materials you are considering for your pupils:

1. Insure that commerical program goals are compatible with your instructional goals.
2. Insure that the commercial program flows smoothly from frame to frame. Do not assume that the pupils will be able to bridge "gaps" in concepts or procedures presented in the program.
3. Insure that the commercial program written materials conform to the independent reading level[1] of pupils who will use the program (reading instruction programs excluded). Good programs carry a statement of the estimated reading level of program materials.

There are at least 3000 commercial programmed learning packages available in this country, and another 2000 in Great Britain. These programs are listed in the occasional catalogs of most major publishers, but complete listings can be found in:

1. Hendershot, Carl. *Programmed Learning: A Bibliography of Programmes and Presentation Devices.* This book provides descriptions and sources of United States Learning Programs. Available from Dr. Carl Hendershot, 4114 Ridgewood Drive, Bay City, Michigan 48787. $11.50.
2. Cavanagh, Peter and Clive Jones. *Yearbook of Educational and Instructional Technology.* This book provides descriptions and sources of British and some U. S. programs. Available from Educational Technology Publications Inc., 140 Sylvan Ave., Englewood Cliffs, N. J. 07632. $7.95.

The programs listed in the Hendershot and the Cavanagh and Jones catalogs include programs designed to teach everything from reading readiness through high school remedial reading, from elementary addition through symbolic logic. There is almost certain to be an existing program of interest to every teacher reading this chapter, regardless of specialty. That there is an existing program appropriate to the instructional goals of every

---

[1] This refers to the Betts definition of *independent reading level*. When a reader achieves a comprehension score of 99 percent or more, and can recognize 90 percent or more of the running vocabulary of a given written selection, then that selection is at, or below, his independent reading level. It is unwise to assume an IRL of more than 7.5 grade level for an average high school group.

teacher reading this chapter is a very different matter. The question of appropriateness must be answered on the basis of individual teacher judgment. We inserted the three guidelines above to aid the judgment.

Preparing Pupils to Pursue Programs

Some elementary and secondary teachers have experienced difficulty with pupil misbehavior and/or pupil boredom when pupils have been set to work with programmed instructional devices. It is our experience that the difficulty has most often been caused by the pupils' inability to read the materials. The reading level of the programs was much greater than the independent reading level of the pupils. The only remedy for this problem is to get a program pupils can read.

It also has happened that programs, chosen in accordance with the three guidelines above, still failed when introduced to pupils. Most often, this difficulty was caused by the lack of pupil preparation to use and accept the programs. This can be overcome through teacher adherence to the following preparatory steps:

1. Persuade pupils to accept program work as worthwhile to the achievement of learning goals each student accepts.
2. Teach pupils how to use the program.
3. Separate evaluations of pupil written responses to the program from report card mark determinations. Base report card mark determinations upon observations of pupil work separate from the program.
4. Discourage pupils from skipping parts of the program. The nature of the programs makes skipping material a self-defeating practice.
5. Give pupils work spaces as free from distraction as possible. Program work is one task that learning carrels were designed for, and these should be used whenever possible.

Sense and Nonsense About Programs

It is conceivable that some educators will have the need, the desire, and the time to write small programs of the linear type to fill gaps in either existing commercial programs, or to add variety to local instruction.

It is inconceivable that any classroom teacher will have anything like the time required to write even small programs on the Intrinsic Branching model.

The main value of this chapter to practicing professionals is a familiarization with two major and effective programing techniques so that those directly involved in education can make sensible evaluations of commercially produced programs now reaching the market. That is sense.

There is a tendency on the part of some publishers to label every workbook or every textbook as a "program." In the way "program" is used in this chapter, that is nonsense. A close reading of this chapter should show that linear teaching programs and Intrinsic Branching teaching programs are highly specialized, amazingly complex teaching aids to the accomplishment of specific academic learning objectives. While the production of workbooks to conform to one of the two programming techniques may be an improvement over the present workbook model, this is not the case for textbooks. Programmed learning is developing as an important supplement to the direct communication format of the textbook, but programmed learning formats are neither intended to replace all textbooks, nor likely to do so.

Major Considerations in Program Use

Three guidelines to teacher program selection suggest that teachers examine program goals, program flow, and program reading level to insure that the program conforms to local working objectives, is reasonable in presenting an unbroken flow of concept development, and that it conforms to the reading level of pupils.

The probability that pupils will accept program work can be increased if the teacher introducing program work will follow the five managerial steps listed above.

14

The Systems Approach to Curriculum
and Instruction

Let's Knock the Mystery out of Systems

A fast disappearing teacher chore is the necessity to maintain a double-entry record of attendance for each child in the class or home room. If you are still keeping an attendance register, you won't be keeping it for long. Administrators have finally discovered that computers love to keep attendance records, and teachers don't. However, since the mechanics of attendance registers are still fresh in your memory, the register will serve as a familiar example of a *system*.

It is deflating to the aura of complexity, wizardry, and mystery presently surrounding the term *system* to call anything as mundane and old fashioned as an attendance register by the same name. However, your old attendance register was a system. It was a system designed to provide you and your boss with a way to accurately account for the presence or absence of every child in your care. It also told you when you counted correctly, and when you were wrong. Furthermore, at stratospheric levels of state school administration, the child accounting information from every school in the state poured in each June in standardized form. Because of the standardized format, beady-eyed child accountants at the state education department could accurately assemble child accounting information for your entire state, and presumably tell the governor how many children were in school last year.

Note that the attendance register, the old child accounting

system, worked without electronic data processing machinery. Child accounting was one of the first chores school administrators turned over to computers, but the *system* for child accounting existed long before electronic data processing existed. You don't need to have a computer to have a *system.*

Most states incorporated simple symbols in their child accounting systems during the attendance register days so that teachers and principals could tell from a glance at the attendance register which children had a string of absences and why. In this way, the system served the purpose of alerting teachers to a problem. It allowed teachers to specifically describe the excessive, unexcused absence problem to an attendance officer or social worker so that steps could be taken to solve the problem. Continued surveillance of the register, after referral, allowed the teacher to evaluate the results of the referral, and to raise cain if the child continued to miss school days for spurious reasons.

The attendance register *system* permitted the teacher to spot and define an attendance problem, prescribe action to solve the problem, observe the action taken, and evaluate the results of the action. If there were no results, the teacher could re-refer the problem and start the definition-prescription-action-evaluation process all over again. Systems devotees call that "recycling in a closed loop," but you don't need to know that much about systems jargon.

How to Identify an Instructional System

You do need to know that the heart of the *instructional system* is the four step sequence:

1. diagnosis of learning problems
2. prescription for corrective action
3. corrective action
4. evaluation of results of corrective action

Of course, these four steps are what a certain breed of educational "expert" has been telling teachers to take since the dawn of the M.Ed. However, many professional have abandoned telling, and started doing by devising instructional systems for their own class or school. Two of these are Sue Logan and Dan Washington.

Sue Logan's Recipe for a Seatwork System

Sue Logan is a fifth-grade teacher in an eastern suburb. A few years ago Sue managed her fifth-grade reading class of twenty-eight pupils in the traditional manner maintaining low, medium, and high achievement groups just like the settings on an electric toaster. She has a small group in level 3 materials, a group using level 4 materials, and a group of children reading in level 5 materials. Sue's pupils were improving some of their reading skills, but she wanted to do more.

Sue was unhappy with the seatwork exercises provided by her basal and supplementary workbooks and dittoed worksheets. She recognized that the workbook exercises were designed to correct some reading problems her pupils didn't even have, and that the exercises were too brief to provide sufficient exercise to correct problems that some pupils did have.

Being something of a pack rat, Sue had an extensive collection of workbooks and ditto masters in her closet at school, and in her attic at home. She sorted out this collection on a rainy Sunday and found she had over fifty different reading workbooks covering four levels of difficulty. Happily, she also had a teacher's manual for many of them, and her principal was able to get most of the teacher's manuals she lacked.

Next, Sue color-coded a portion of the page edges of each workbook with the same color she had marked the accompanying teacher's manual. She did this so that when color and page number matched, between teacher's manual page and workbook (or worksheet) page, the exercise answers could easily be found.

With this done, Sue unstapled and unglued the pupil workbooks to free the pages. Most of the workbooks had a key to the main objective for each exercise, and Sue used these keys to sort the pages into categories according to objectives. Many pages were designed to meet more than a single objective, and Sue categorized these in the objectives groupings she needed most.

Soon Sue had a pile of thirty different workbook pages designed to exercise children in applying the double consonant syllabification generalization. She would have had more, but she had only one copy of most of the dissected workbooks, and she lost some syllabification exercises to more valuable exercises on the reverse of the page. She placed her double consonant syllabification exercises pages in an appropriately marked file folder. This was the first of many file folders identified as containing "outlining skills exercises," "alphabetizing skills exercises," "reading for a specific purpose exercises," and so on through the catalog of reading skills.

Two months after that rainy Sunday, Sue carried a box of sixty file folders containing an organized set of reading exercises to her classroom. She taught her pupils how to get a page from the file, a way to complete the page requirements on a separate sheet of paper, a way to return the workbook page to the proper file folder, and to check their own work by referring to one of the color coded teacher's manuals. Now, at the termination of a reading lesson, Sue could direct each child to a specific file folder to work to improve the reading skill that he needed at the time.

This was Sue's *system*. It was incomplete in that there was no systematic procedure for problem diagnosis. Sue still relied on occasional tests and a teacher "feel" for that. Sue prescribed worksheet exercises by simply telling each child what he was to work on. No system there, either. For problem correction, Sue had a system. Her initial, systematized collection of cut-up workbooks and the procedure for children to use them worked smoothly, and Sue doubled her collection in two years. Sue also had some control of evaluation. She double checked the children's self-correction on a periodic basis, and her observation of the self-corrected papers told her when and how a child was progressing. Whenever a child had great difficulty with a series of worksheets, Sue knew what his problem was from the worksheet category titles. She then made it a point to speak to the problem in small group instructional sessions.

Sue Logan's system, though a partial system, provided her pupils with independent reading exercises pointed to pupil needs. It also freed her of the managerial task of distributing, collecting, and checking workbook exercises. She could have built a diagnostic component into the system through construction of an informal reading inventory keyed to her filing system categories. This would have provided a basis for teacher prescriptive decisions, and would have brought her system to meet the four criteria of an instructional system.

Dan Washington's Recipe for a Supplementary System

Dan Washington taught psychology in a large midwestern high school. Dan's course stood high in the school status system, and he had little problem with student motivation. However, he did have some trouble finding suitable instructional materials. To meet the materials problem, Dan devised "mini-systems" to augment the student textbook in spots where Dan knew the book to be weak. For example, early in Dan's text he perceived an inadequate treatment of defense mechanisms.

Dan's text provided a brief description of six defense mechanisms (rationalization, reaction formation, isolation, denial, undoing, and projection). Later, the Text assumed that students had developed an understanding of the mechanisms as text material provided explanations of various human relations difficulties. Dan supplemented his textbook by devising a little instructional system to help students gain an understanding of the six defense mechanisms.

The teacher-made materials part of Dan's system consisted of eighteen sample social situations written like drama scripts. Each script illustrated a situation wherin overuse of one of the defense mechanisms resulted in a breakdown of communications between two or more people. Dan wrote three different scripts dramatizing each defense mechanism.

Early in the course, Dan provided his students with a short lecture designed to familiarize them with the mechanisms. Next, he directed pupils to read the textbook segment dealing with defense mechanisms. When the students completed the reading, Dan engaged the group in a teacher-pupil discussion of the mechanisms, and of a project for helping pupils build their familiarity with the mechanisms into knowledge and understanding. To aid this process, Dan directed his pupils to divide themselves into work groups of three or four students. Each group of students selected a set of scripts dealing with one of the defense mechanisms. Following a careful re-reading of the textbook segment on defenses, plus a reading and independent student discussion of the scripts, each group of students was to write an original script illustrating an overuse of the defense mechanism described by their script packet. This independent, small group activity culminated in a dramatization of the original scripts by each student group. Following each dramatization, viewing students tried to guess which defense mechanism had been dramatized. The dramatizations resulted in some lively teacher-student and student-student interaction sessions as players tried to defend their presentations, while viewers argued the ambiguity of the actions. Dan's students were defining for themselves the limits of the defense mechanism concepts. The post-drama sessions also provided Dan with feedback on his pupils' understanding of the six defense mechanisms.

When the teacher-student interaction sessions satisfied Dan that his pupils had sufficient understanding of the defense mechanisms to allow them to use the concepts to make sense of the rest of the text book, Dan returned to a traditional read text-lecture-discuss material presentation of subsequent materials.

Dan's *system* for bringing his pupils to understand the defense mechanisms is diagrammed in Figure 14-1.

Dan's system began with his *diagnosis* that most, probably all, pupils needed more exposure to the specifics of the six defense mechanisms than were provided by the traditional read-lecture-discuss procedure he customarily utilized. Dan's *prescription for corrective action* involved independent pupil reading of his scripts, group pupil activity in making and dramatizing original scripts, person-to-person interactions among pupils to determine the mechanism dramatized, and extensive pupil-to-pupil interaction in attacking or defending the accuracy of the dramatizations. During the last phase of the *corrective action* Dan had an opportunity to *evaluate* the results of his system. If he was satisfied that pupils had gained an understanding of the defense mechanism concepts, then he moved back to his traditional means for presenting future material. However, if he was not satisfied that pupils understood the concepts, then he could return students to the start of his mini-system (dotted line on Figure 14-1), and repeat the defense mechanism exposition.

If Dan's system sounds something like the Intrinsic Branching programing technique discussed in Chapter 13, then you know something about systems and programming. A learning program is a little system, but a system does not need to include programmed learning. It can, but it doesn't have to.

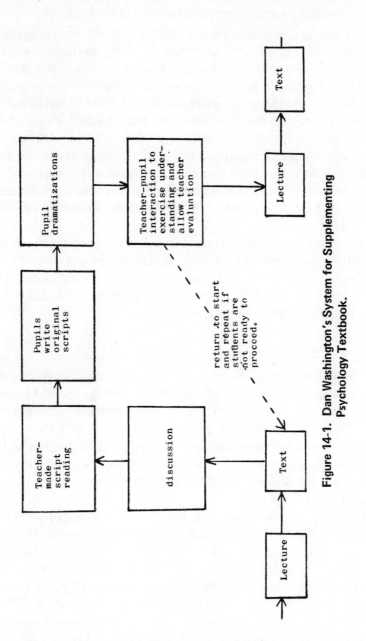

Figure 14-1. Dan Washington's System for Supplementing Psychology Textbook.

Commercial Systems Presently in Your School

Many professionals realize that some of the materials from educational publishers are built on the systems model. The *Reading Laboratories* pioneered by Science Research Associates incorporate the diagnosis-prescription-corrective action-evaluation steps that characterize systems. SRA and other major publishers have produced boxes similar to the *Reading Labs* providing self-contained and self-sustaining systems for teaching mathematics, English, geography, economics, civics, and social studies. Physical Science Study Committee, Chemical Education Materials Study, and Biological Sciences Curriculum Study produced packages are also examples of ready-made instructional systems available, and in use.

The teacher-made instructional systems based on the diagnosis-prescription-corrective action-evaluation model are the least complex instructional systems. Next, in complexity, are the publisher produced packages exemplified by SRA Labs and the National Science Foundation inspired systems ·

Machine Based Systems

The most complex, and most comprehensive instructional systems require some type of machine to manage record keeping and a series of programs. Usually these systems incorporate the teacher, instructional programs, and machine in a closely coordinated man-machine instructional setting. The teacher acts as a humanizing and integrating force in the system, and the machine-program handles the details, particularly the reinforcement giving, and record keeping details.

A well conceived machine based system incorporates the same four principles that characterize all systems. However, the machine based systems provide for far more thorough pupil diagnosis than a teacher working alone can provide. The machine based systems also provide more, and more varied, learning programs designed to tailor instruction to learner characteristics than are usually available to individual classroom teachers or teaching teams. For example, one computer based system produced by the Harvard University Computing Center provides a way for the teacher to diagnose pupil instructional needs on the basis of pupil readiness, learning style, estimated ability, personality, and past achieve-ment. The system allows the teacher to direct pupils to the learning program best suited to each individual pupil on the basis of the five variables. Moreover, as the variables change, the system alerts the teacher to the changes, and provides the teacher with materials appropriate to the changes. That's individualization with a vengeance.

Teachers and administrators in schools where machine based systems are now operational are aware of the benefits from, and difficulties inherent in machine based instructional systems oper-ation. If you are not among the growing group of systems users, don't scoff and say, "It can't happen here." Machine based systems use is growing, and very soon systems will, at least, "be considered here."

Six Steps to Selecting Systems

The selection of a commercial system, not dependent upon a machine for operation, may be a one teacher or one principal selection job. The six steps listed below will aid selection. The selection of a machine based instructional system must include many teachers and administrators due to the large scope of such systems, and to the large initial expenditures of time and money in installing them. Nevertheless, the six steps for systems selection are the same for both situations. Only the scope of the selection operation is larger for machine based systems.

The first step to selecting any system is deciding, and defining precisely what you want to accomplish. Stating school objectives as working objectives is an essential first step to systems selection. It is an essential first step to even considering machine based instructional systems.

Next, you need to know what is available. The materials information retrieval system described in Chapter 7 will identify the publishers of systems not dependent upon machines. These systems are widely advertised by their publishers. Present and prospective users of machine based systems will find the *Index to Computer Assisted Instruction* [1] an indispensible guide to both hardware and software for machine based instructional systems.

---

[1] Lekan, Helen A. (ed.) *Index to Computer Assisted Instruction.* Available from Sterling Institute, 3750 Prudential Tower, Boston, Massachusetts 02199. $19.50.

The Lekan *Index* lists 214 computer based systems for mathematics instruction alone. The math instructional systems cover pupil achievement levels from first grade through graduate school. The *Index* also lists 31 computer based reading systems designed to teach learners as diverse as kindergarten toddlers and adult executives. The *Index* lists one or more computer based instructional systems at least touching on every subject treated in your school.

The third step in choosing a commercial system, machine based or otherwise, is to compare your class or school objectives with the objectives of the system. A well integrated system cannot be used selectively, like a textbook. In almost all cases you either use the system whole, or leave it alone. Therefore, if you find that your objectives clash with some of the instructional system objectives, you had better find another system. Even the simple process of matching school objectives with system objectives is difficult in evaluating machine based systems. It is wise to employ one of the systems analyst school consultants listed in the Lekan *Index* to assist in this activity.

The fourth step is a consideration of system flexibility. Non-machine based systems are usually designed for a specific purpose, such as arithmetic instruction, covering three or four achievement levels. Due to the low cost of these systems, great flexibility is not provided, but they should make provision for several achievement levels. However, high cost machine based systems should offer great software acceptance flexiblity. Unfortunately, there is a lack of standardization in the machine based instructional systems field, and it is often the case if you purchase the hardware of a certain manufacturer, you are limited to the use of only that manufacturer's software in the system. You may find a system so ideally matched to your pupils' present and assumed future instructional needs that you are willing to give-up flexibility to get the system. Nevertheless, remember that this action commits you to a single software producer for a long time. Flexibility, the feature allowing use of many manufacturers' software on a single machine, is a desirable feature.

Step five is a careful evaluation of the specific systems that profess to match your objectives and your need for flexibility. The diagnosis part of the system must be credible to you and your colleagues. For example, if you mistrust standardized personality tests *in toto,* then avoid systems which use personality tests as one diagnostic tool. Be sure you agree with the instruments used to define and isolate diagnostic variables. The prescription and corrective action components of the system also need to be analyzed to determine your agreement that the student activities prescribed are likely to lead to the stated objectives of the system. Finally, the evaluation criteria need to be inspected. Systems which prescribe only pupil drill on questions listed in the evaluative criteria part of the system are more "conditioning systems" than instructional systems. Look for evaluative criteria that stress pupil use of concepts, processes, and attitudes rather than criteria dependent upon pupil memorization of "right answers."

For decisions concerning machine based systems, we recommend a sixth, "try before you buy" evaluative step. Producers of systems will not usually set-up an instructional system in your school on a trial basis. However, you can locate a school using the specific machine based system that you like, and arrange to send a dozen or so pupils and several teachers to that school during a low use summer period. This group can sample things such as ease of hardware operation, pupil interest in instructional materials, clarity of system teacher directions, and supporting equipment requirements. Travel, salary, and maintenance costs for a dozen pupils, and several teachers for a five or six week systems trial in a distant city will be negligible compared to the cost of installing a machine based instructional system that fails to work for your school or school district.

A Final Word on Systems

The teacher's attendance register is an example of a system. It aided teachers in identifying problems, defining problems, prescribing problem solving action, observing action, and evaluating results of action. Problem definition, prescription, problem solving action, and results evaluation are the characteristics of any system.

Instructional systems make provision for these four steps by providing for diagnosis, prescription, corrective action, and evaluation of learning.

Instructional systems can be as simple as Sue Logan's reading system, and as complex as Harvard University's computer assisted instructional system.

The systems approach to curriculum and instruction can aid professionals in the rational planning, implementation, and evaluation of instruction on the basis of what each pupil needs, rather than on the basis of what the textbook says. Professionals should view the comprehensive instructional systems as offering a practical way to reconcile the ideal of individualized instruction with the reality of the thirty-to-one pupil-teacher ratio.

15

Splitters and Lumpers

The Splitter Emphasis

Leland Jacobs, the venerable Columbia University professor of education, is fond of dividing educators into two archetypes: "splitters" and "lumpers." For Dr. Jacobs, the "splitters" are those who insist upon breaking-down the learning process into tiny, definable, analyzable steps. "Splitters" can suffer from an excess of logic, and a deficit of the feel for other human beings that has made Mark Hopkins and his log the ideal of personalized, humanized education.

This book has placed great emphasis upon "splitter" devices such as levels of learning, principles of learning psychology, a systems approach to curriculum development, managerial and substantive goals, models of learning, specific teaching methods, a procedure for interaction analysis, linear and intrinsic branching programing, and structured instructional systems.

Reconciling Splitter Techniques with Lumper Goals

These devices are not intended to make machines out of teachers, or intellectual hamburger out of pupils. The devices are simply tools. We hope that these powerful teaching tools will be used professionally to help "lumpers," like Carol, get out of the closet and into warm contacts with children. The devices can give the world's Joan Welds and Keith Sloanes time to get off the lecture platform, and settled on a log in a human to human lumper relationship with one or two pupils. Used in this way the tools of the splitters can provide lumpers with the time they need to reflect with pupils on the meaning of the great lumps of connected reality such as man, and nature, and God, and love.

These are heady topics for children and adolescents, but not out of reach when sensitive lumpers understand that what Sam Hudson's teacher said about art instruction applies also to the art of guiding pupils to confront great issues. Let this book end with that art teacher's retort to Sam, "You have to teach them something first."

INDEX

INDEX

217